The Contemporary Violinist

by Julie Lyonn Lieberman

The Contemporary Violinist

by Julie Lyonn Lieberman

Published by:

Huiksi Music

Post Office Box 495

New York, NY 10024 U.S.A.

Graphic Design: Julie Lyonn Lieberman

Cover Design: Loren Moss

Cover Photo: Randall Wallace

Editor: Susan Ruel

You can reach Julie Lyonn Lieberman c/o:

http://members.aol.com/julielyonn

Table of Contents

The Practice CD

Practice the tunes in the book using these tracks. Each accompaniment provides the melody and ample space for improvisation.

Julie Lyonn Lieberman: violin
Len Cascia: guitar, accordion, mandolin, pedal steel
Alex Skolnick: flamenco, bebop, and blues guitar
Steve Alcott: bass

Preface

It's a great time to be studying the violin. String players have finally reached the point in their daily musical lives where American popular styles and indigenous music from around the world are part of the ubiquitous whole, and no longer the exclusive province of specialized and somewhat lonely innovators. From the orchestra to the recording studio, violinists, violists, and cellists are expected to have a working understanding of the wonderful rhythmic musical melange available to the public every day.

So broad is the palette and daunting the challenge that well-designed new methods and materials for study are desperately needed.

From violinists Leopold Mozart in the 18th century to Leopold Auer in the 19th and early 20th, string pedagogy has experienced a continually evolving and innovative development as it has responded to the demands of composers and their Euro-centric vision. But for most of this past century we have simply been refining this albeit excellent methodology and virtually mass-producing a singular technique that is designed to accommodate a singular style: classical music.

Today, however, music calls out for more.

Necessity must again be a mother of invention. Multifarious improvisation in jazz, rock, folk swing, bebop, bossa nova, samba, mambo, salsa, bluegrass, Balkan rhythms, Irish fiddle, Cajun, hip-hop, new age, blues, and R&B styles....it's all available for exploration. There is no reason for string players to feel 'left out' 'too stiff' or 'too classical' and miss the joy of this musical evolution. They should have the flexibility and comfort that horn players and guitarists have always enjoyed. We Turtle Islanders can tell you from first-hand experience that there is a ton of fun to be had when you start to stretch.

None of this will come as any surprise to anyone who has been paying attention the past few years to our esteemed friend and colleague violinist/educator Julie Lyonn Lieberman. She has always known this day was coming and has been preparing us all with incomparably useful, inspiring books, and an unshakable commitment to finding better ways to learn. **The Contemporary Violinist** is perhaps the most comprehensive and informative yet. For the uninitiated student it is a portal to a new world. For the already informed it will open eyes wide to new possibilities. Grab it and USE it!

-Turtle Island String Quartet

Special thanks to my husband, Len Cascia, for his love, support, and help with this project.

Very special thanks to those who went the extra mile:

Turtle Island String Quartet, Loren Moss, Susan Ruel, Pete Schug, Leif Alpsjö, Yale Strom, Alicia Svigals, Mary Larsen, Lourds, Alex Skolnick, and Steve Alcott.

I would also like to thank all of the phenomenal artists who gave of their time and expertise to add the richness of their experience to this book: Jean-Luc Ponty, Buddy Spicher, Mary Ann Harbar, Matt Glaser, James Kelly, Martin Hayes, Bruce Molsky, Jay Ungar, Mark Wood, Betsy Hill, Joe Kennedy, Jr., John Hartford, Randy Sabien, Claude Williams, Richard Greene, Stacy Phillips, Darol Anger, Michael Doucet, Leif Alpsjö, Yale Strom, Alicia Svigals, Willie Royal, Donna Hébert, Natalie MacMaster, Papa John Creach, Anthony Barnett, Susan Ruel, Dave Barton, Betsy Kubick, and Sam Zygmuntowicz.

Special thanks to my cousin, Janet (Schneider) Stoddard, whose artwork in this book helps keep her forever alive and present in the world.

Introduction

"Julie, I feel so confused. I don't know if I'm a bluegrass fiddler, a swing violinist, or a composer. I don't know what to focus on any more." Though some of the styles named vary, I hear this a lot nowadays. And I certainly was guilty of the same statement when I started on the path of the contemporary violinist in the early 70s.

The purist who can say, "I'm a classical violinist," or "I'm an Irish fiddler" may be today's dinosaur. And when I meet someone and tell them that I'm a violinist, I'm no longer constantly met with "What orchestra do you play in?" or strange stares if I describe myself as an improvising violinist. It's in our culture now.

When the editor of my first book, **Blues Fiddle**, asserted that the book probably wouldn't sell because we weren't talking about the surf at Malibu but more like a blip at Coney Island, I told him he was wrong...that we were talking about the future. That was in 1976.

Please don't misunderstand me. I highly respect all traditional musicians, whether they play old-time fiddle or Greek violin. They are messengers who transport cultural soundscapes of the past into the future. I also celebrate the new kind of player who is developing creative contributions and fearless explorations to keep the art playfully alive.

The future is at our doorstep and my vision is of the contemporary violinist. One who knows fiddle styles (Irish, bluegrass, old time, Scandinavian, Cajun, country, et al.); can improvise in any style; greets odd meter such as 5/8 or 11/8 with expertise; can play rhythm violin; wails on the blues with lightning and thunder, and is equally at home with the classics.

It's a new identity that embraces diversity. As our world gets smaller, perhaps we can be among the leaders exemplifying human possibilities in the next century.

Dedication

This book is dedicated to Claude "Fiddler" Williams.

It was his 1972 solo on "Hootie Blues" on an album with Jay McShann that inspired me to write my **Blues Fiddle** book back in the 70s. In 1984, I presented Claude at the Third American Jazz String Summit. He turned the place upside down and inside out. I found name jazz violinists hiding in the dressing room afterwards, each one standing in a corner with their instrument, madly trying to figure out what they had just heard. That evening I'd introduced Claude with a song I'd written for him titled "Fiddle Down," reflecting my sadness that he'd spent decades in relative obscurity; I felt that his talent deserved immense public recognition. At that time, there weren't any albums available featuring him as a solo artist, so I released a live recording of his set at the Summit to try to turn the tide.

After writing an article on Claude for STRINGS Magazine, I was instrumental in his debut on Charles Kuralt's *Sunday Morning CBS News* in an interview with Billy Taylor. I could never do enough for him. I think that many of his admirers in the jazz violin world feel the same way, as does his longtime friend and manager, Russ Dantzler. The outpouring of articles, workshops, and concerts created on a grassroots level by admirers such as Matt Glaser, John Blake Jr., and Mark O'Connor, testify to how deeply he is appreciated and loved.

Though I thoroughly enjoyed being his "date" at the opening party for his debut on Broadway in *Black and Blue* (don't worry, his wife knew), one of my favorite jaunts with Claude was when I took him and John Blake Jr. to visit legendary jazz bassist Milt Hinton at Milt's home. In the presence of two living legends, the four of us spent the afternoon watching Milt's homemade movies of Joe Venuti, and looking at his photos of Eddie South, Stuff Smith, and a few obscure violinists from Chicago whose names escape me now.

Claude's contribution to the field of jazz violin, his open door policy to younger players, and his gentle soul has enriched all of our lives immeasurably in the string community and the world.

Jay McShann and Claude "Fiddler" Williams

Fiddle Down that long sweet road now. Fiddle Down 90 years or more now.
Fiddle Down that lonesome road, but here we are to hear you play.
Fiddle Down from your soul now. Fiddle Down to make us whole now. Fiddle down,
we love you so, that here we are to hear you play! Fiddle Down…

The fiddle, like all musical instruments, is part of your voice and therefore a window into everything you are and wish to be; so that each style on the fiddle could be thought of as a language. And therefore, to play old time music, or Cajun music or Mexican or classical or whatever, you've got to learn the language. Language has subtleties and therefore many layers. A player can just learn an old-time tune and to some-one who doesn't already know the language it will sound old timey but to someone else who is familiar with the dialects and the metaphors it would sound much like someone with a thick foreign accent speaking their native tongue. The violin/fiddle is such a sensitive instrument with so many variables that the depth you can get to (in any style/language) is bottomless.

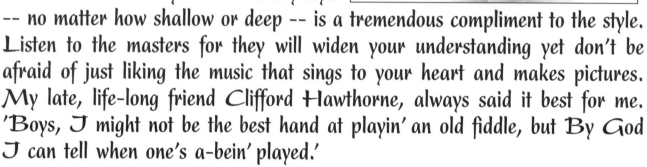

I believe that to try and learn any style -- no matter how shallow or deep -- is a tremendous compliment to the style. Listen to the masters for they will widen your understanding yet don't be afraid of just liking the music that sings to your heart and makes pictures. My late, life-long friend Clifford Hawthorne, always said it best for me. 'Boys, I might not be the best hand at playin' an old fiddle, but By God I can tell when one's a-bein' played.'

- John Hartford

Getting Started

Capturing Style

Each of the units in this book focuses on a different style as a vehicle for improvisation. Much the way the English language can be spoken with dozens of different accents, depending upon where in the country one travels, the individual musician can create a stylistic "accent" on their instrument through imitation. We are actually learning to emulate the accepted sounds of a culture or subculture, adapting ourselves to an idea that we have agreed to adopt as our own about what music should or shouldn't sound like.

We have five basic parameters to work with in each hand that help define our sound. How we mirror or mix and match the two hands multiplies our sound palette.

Notation truly fails us when it comes to the range of expressive dynamics available to us while playing. Take a line of eighth notes as an example. On paper they will look the same, yet each note can be cheated of its full time value, lilted, dragged, or swung. Listen to the style you are interested in, learning as much as you can to master its inflection.

Also keep in mind that arrangement and instrumentation help define style. Playing a tune against varying rhythmic settings or with a banjo player versus a percussionist or an accordionist, will impact the overall effect the music has on its listeners.

If you want to really get inside a music connected with a specific culture, get inside the culture. Find a master teacher from that culture. Failing that, find the oldest, authentic recordings of the style. The history of the violin in salsa, swing, bluegrass and country are all well documented on record.

There are many levels of playing these musics. Really absorbing a style means you should be able to play it "freely" without slipping out of the style. That does **not** mean merely playing some typical embellishments. If you really understand it, you should be able to play the style without resorting to such sign posts as a cut in an Irish tune, or a slide into a third degree in a blues tune.

- **Stacy Phillips**

The Five Basic Parameters:

1) pressure

Subtle variations in pressure can add different expressive qualities to your playing. To gain control of how the bow interacts with the string, you must keep your hand flexible. All of your fingers need to be relaxed and curved. If a single finger is stiff, straight, or locked, it will be extremely difficult to achieve subtlety in your sound. You will then have to turn to the large muscles of the arm to try to regulate bow weight, which is an inefficient use of your musculature.

2) speed

You can draw a fast long bow or a slow short bow on the same length note and create completely different effects. Keep in mind that your strings offer their greatest resistance when you bow closer to the bridge, so this is where you will need to guide your bow if moving it slowly; a faster bow will need to be placed further away from the bridge. Experiment with and allow the sound to teach you where your bow needs to be placed for each effect.

3) duration

The length of time you hold a note, slide into it, or add an ornament to it can also add a lot of flavor. Learning how to change note length, yet not speed up or slow down the pulse of the music, is a challenge. If you end a note early, you must learn how to fill the extra space with silence; if you hold a note slightly longer than written, you must make up for that by shortening the next note(s). The idea is to keep the overall measure or phrase length the same, and to keep the pulse steady enough to dance to.

4) & 5) method of entry, and
method of departure

Pay attention to how you start and end notes and phrases, and experiment with the difference between sudden changes versus gradual ones. This requires subtle control so don't get frustrated if you don't get the results you want immediately!

OUR NERVOUS SYSTEM IS RIGGED SUCH THAT ONE SIDE OF THE BODY AUTOMATICALLY WILL TEND TO MIMIC THE OTHER SIDE. THE MORE YOU CAN ISOLATE WHAT EACH HAND DOES AND DEVELOP ITS SKILLS INDEPENDENT OF THE OTHER HAND, THE MORE CHOICES YOU WILL HAVE WHEN IT COMES TO CREATING A PALETTE OF WIDELY VARIED SOUNDS. FOR INSTANCE, YOU CAN LIGHTEN PRESSURE AND SPEED UP THE MOTION OF THE BOW TO MATCH A FAST SLIDE, OR USE A SLOW, HEAVY BOW AS THE LEFT HAND SLIDES LIGHTLY AND QUICKLY.

Dressing Up A Note

As we discussed in the unit "Capturing Style," there are an immeasurable number of ways to play just one note by using variations in attack, pressure, speed, duration, and termination. You can color each note further through the use of ornamentation, either by how you "dress it up" with the left hand (using grace notes, turns, trills, etc.) or with the right hand (bounced bow, chop technique, the Irish triplet, tremolo, and so on).

The problem with trying to discuss or notate ornamentation is that most of these sounds are comprised of split second changes in coordination between the two hands that often can't be captured on paper. Supplement your practice with a great deal of listening. Choose recordings from the area of the world you most wish to incorporate into your playing, and try to emulate what you hear.

I have shaped a group of notes into a short melodic line to demonstrate how they might be played in a few of the styles represented in this book. Let's see if you can identify which style is which! Use *Track One: Stylistic Examples* on the practice CD to help you shape your sound appropriately.

Passionate Technique

While talking about kinesthetic awareness during a presentation of my "Playing Healthy" seminar in Alabama, a student responded, "Well, I just force myself to play several hours of etudes every day. I ignore how I feel to make it through. Then I reward myself at the end by playing a piece of music. And that's how I get ahead."

Where did he learn to cheat himself of the daily opportunity to be in the company of the beauty and the power of the great musical ocean? Of the chance to express his innermost worlds? Of the possibility of building his own uniquely individual artistry? Of the sheer joy that comes from being present while playing the instrument one's heart has chosen?

Perhaps it is how we are rigged that contributes most to our ability to supercede all stimuli, focus on a goal, and hammer our way toward it no matter what. But then what is it that we've created once we "get there?" And where is "there" if we haven't imbued that process with our individuality, our sensitivity, our full presence?

Aren't we then teaching ourselves to disassociate our physical actions from all of who we are? This is ironic given the fact that most of us hunger to make music as a path toward greater expression and a deeper experience of who we are.

I would like to propose a different path for building technique. It's one in which you breathe, feel, listen deeply, and take your time. Experience each sound you make as music rather than a means toward an end. It's a process where, when you get frustrated and impatient, and wish you could play faster and better, you can pause and give thanks for what you can do, for the opportunity to make music, take a deep breath, and get back into the enjoyment of making music. When we make this mental adjustment, our muscles actually relax and are better able to give us what we want.

After all, how can the music sing if the singer is absent? How can the music breathe if the player isn't?

WE HAVE THE ABILITY TO SEND TECHNICALLY PRECISE DIRECTIONS FROM OUR MOTOR CORTEX VIA OUR NERVES THROUGH THE CENTRAL NERVOUS SYSTEM OUT TO OUR MUSCLES (EFFERENT) THEREBY ACHIEVING MECHANICALLY PERFECT MOTION, YET TREATING THE HANDS AND ARMS AS LITTLE MORE THAN SERVANTS; WE ALSO HAVE THE ABILITY TO RECEIVE INCOMING INFORMATION BY BEING KINESTHETICALLY AWARE (AFFERENT) WHICH WILL ENABLE US TO MONITOR HOW WE ARE USING OUR BODIES, THEREBY GIVING US THE ABILITY TO MAKE SUBTLE BUT IMPORTANT CHANGES IN THE QUALITY OF EXPERIENCE WE CREATE IN OUR MUSCLES.

The Bucking Bronco Syndrome

Picture a guy on a wild horse in the ring. His goal is to stay on for as many seconds as possible. His legs are strong, but that isn't enough. In order to hold on for as long as possible, there has to be a level of will and concentration involved that transcends the wild spirit of the horse

I don't think that there's a single human being who's born with the ability to focus for long periods of time. Full concentration is like a muscle that has potential but can't actualize its potential until it is trained. Think of it like a zone the brain can shift into, floating on the waves of immersion without anything else but the activity existing. Some people meditate to achieve a higher level of mental mastery; others, by the sheer nature of working in emergency situations, learn to develop it; some people go to the casino to enjoy this full immersion; some bike 100 miles up a mountain; some watch television; and then there's us.

There are a few impediments to this glorious mental state besides stamina. Sometimes wires go out of phase, there's a momentary blip and the balloon crashes, leaving us bewildered and annoyed (particularly in the middle of a performance). Then there is our motor cortex's ability to learn sequences of motion like zillions of tiny barcodes that are fed per second to our muscle fiber. The muscle memory that we've built in through hours and hours of practice enables us to think of many other things while playing. Depending upon what we think about, this could be great for mechanical skill but not great for achieving zone-hood.

There are a number of ways to monitor and develop deeper concentration. For instance, bow an open string for ten minutes. Notice how long you can stay completely focussed on listening without thinking about anything. Just listening. Try to extend that sequence of time. If you can only last five seconds, don't get discouraged. That's normal at first. The zone-hood muscle is building strength while the wild horse is bucking.

If you're working on a piece of music or a warm-up exercise, notice how long you can stay totally focussed on whatever task is at hand -- again, without thinking about outside activities, what to have for dinner, and who said what yesterday. Make a note to yourself of where in the tune or exercise you get thrown off the horse. The next day, try to go past that spot. As your ability to focus becomes stronger, you will be able to stay totally immersed for longer and longer periods of time.

How do you know when you've been thrown off the horse? You're having mental conversations with people, looping over something that's happened or is about to happen, daydreaming, or worrying. How do you know when you're in the zone? Your breathing is regular (not held); you are listening 100% to every detail, every nuance, as if through a huge magnifying glass, all the while coaching yourself technically and musically in whatever ways you need to achieve your best playing. And when you get really good at it, it feels like there is absolutely no effort involved!

Erasing the Glass Ceiling

During the learning process, it's quite common to reach a plateau and remain there for various lengths of time. Most artists feel frustrated by this and either briefly decrease (or stop) practice or try harder. The increase in effort often creates muscular tension, which will yield little progress and potential injury, and the "vacation" might be relaxing, but then you aren't making music, are you?

Changing how you practice is the key to consistent movement forward. We tend to initiate activities using thought and movement patterns that are the most familiar because the brain was designed to economize; it's geared to process information over and over in exactly the same manner just because it's easier. Developing a whole new routing pattern isn't a physiological preference. But this often places a limit on how fast and how much we can grow in a given period of time. And learning new cognitive patterns often feels frustrating to adults, so they give up quickly. But it's well worth doing a little bit each day, until these new thinking skills are native to you, rather than getting stuck in a rut.

Multidimensional practice can maximize your practice time by rallying and training all centers of your brain to come to your assistance simultaneously.

Audiation

Listen to a musical phrase in your mind, sing it, and then play it.

Right-Brain Processing

Now close your eyes and image playing that same phrase. Imaging involves experiencing it as if you're doing it, but without moving your body. Include quality of experience, such as deep breathing, good tone, relaxed hands, and any other physical aspects you would like to create in your technique, as you play each note mentally. If you get stuck, play that part of the tune on your instrument, and then image playing it. Too difficult at first? Break it down into a couple of notes at a time.

Left-Brain Processing

Analyze the phrase for relationships. How many half or whole steps were there between the notes? Do the notes form any kind of recognizable pattern? Do the notes conform to the chord tones (1 3 5 or 1 3 5 7) of a key or to a part of a scale? How is the second half of the phrase or tune similar to or different from the first half?

NOTE: Do not play through your mistakes! If you stop each time you make a mistake on a new tune, and go through the three steps outlined above, playing slowly and musically, you will save yourself hours of correction later and improve your overall sound.

> INSANITY IS DOING THE SAME THING OVER AND OVER AGAIN AND EXPECTING DIFFERENT RESULTS.
>
> - ALBERT EINSTEIN

When David Balakrishnan and I were composing and arranging for our group the Turtle Island String Quartet, we talked about using the Joseph Campbell method: find the deep common elements of disparate musical styles and use them to write your own music. This is different from trying to smash together styles for shock or novelty. For instance, the slurs and slides of Celtic music, and its melodic emphasis, correspond deeply with the more classicized and codified sounds of Indian classical music. And the bluesy pitch and funky rhythms of African-American Delta blues share a surprising emotional ground with some Korean music.

This kind of commonality is a crucial factor in the human musical experience, as in myth and religion, which Joseph Campbell explored to our great enrichment. To tease out profound soul connections across musical continents takes time and contemplation and a respect for the fine grain of these forms. And the emotional openness of a fool ... a fiddlin' fool!

- Darol Anger

Regina Carter, Johnny Frigo, Matt Glaser, Joe Kennedy, Jr., and Darol Anger.

The Art of Improvisation

Yikes! What Should I Play?

All of the styles outlined in this book can be used as vehicles for improvisation. Many beginning improvisers say, "I don't know what to play." Play something! Anything! Be willing to make mistakes. It is through your mistakes that you will be able to quickly identify the sounds that you like and the ones you wish to avoid in the future.

Why do students sit in the same area of the classroom class after class when given open seating? Why would someone stay in a relationship or job that is unhealthy or repulsive to them? Let's face it. Humans love familiarity. The safety it provides often outweighs one's heart's desire for improvement or change. But many times the contemplation of and the first few moments of change are the hardest part. Then we wonder why we waited so long.

If you have spent your entire musical life memorizing tunes by ear or only playing what your eyes tell you to play through reading notated music, then improvisation -- no matter how alluring -- can feel uncomfortable and intimidating. You've also undoubtedly spent all of those years investing enormous energy and time into avoiding making any mistakes. And obsessing when you did.

Mistakes can be used as doorways to discovery.

When you improvise you get to select a sequence of pitches that are pleasing to you. There are actually 5,042 possible combinations of a seven-note scale! How you rhythmize and colorize the notes you select using textures, slides, or ornamentation, helps create your individual sound. Getting started with this seemingly colossal journey is easy. Summon the child in you who loved to explore, experiment and play -- before you learned to "be an adult" -- and start by playing one note until you love how it sounds and then find another one. And another.

A mistake is only a half step away from the right note.
– Betty Carter

If you play something that you don't like, play it again with gusto and then move gracefully to a neighboring pitch. Remind yourself on a regular basis that it's just as important to explore new right-hand textures, rhythms, and emotional contours as it is to develop interesting melodic phrases with your fingering hand.

Even if you aren't interested in becoming a full-time improvising violinist, improvisation will teach you how to listen more deeply. Since the visual cortex in the brain is larger than and tends to dominate the auditory cortex, reading musicians rarely have the opportunity to experience pure listening sessions on a daily basis. Each time you improvise, you will be strengthening your listening.

There is a second listening skill developed during improvisation. It is called audiation. This is when you hear a musical phrase in your inner ear and externalize it on your instrument. This advanced form of ear training can assist you in learning composed music as well, because your ability to retain and play melodic lines will improve.

As you practice improvising, experiment by trying to focus on creating some of the following approaches:

♪ - tell a story

♪ - create a melodic line

♪ - welcome silence

♪ - listen listen listen …

You can also use different types of improvisational parameters to develop your skills.

Try creating …

♪ - a one-minute improvisation

♪ - a one-note improvisation using texture and rhythm to evoke musical definition

♪ - a two-note improvisation

♪ - long tones, only changing pitch when you hear the next pitch in your inner ear

♪ - sing and then play the line you've sung

If you laugh self-consciously, create an improvisation based on the different sounds of laughter!

IMPROVISING MUSICIANS ACTUALLY BALANCE A NUMBER OF MENTAL SKILLS SIMULTANEOUSLY. I CALL THIS WHOLE-BRAIN MUSIC-MAKING: THE LEFT BRAIN (LINEAR, SEQUENTIAL) MUST REMEMBER THE SEQUENCE OF CHORDS IN THE PROPER ORDER; MEANWHILE THE RIGHT BRAIN (CREATIVE), IS INVENTING NEW MUSICAL PHRASES WHILE MAPPING EACH KEY ACROSS THE FINGERBOARD (SPATIAL) THROUGH A THREE-DIMENSIONAL IMAGE; THE FINGERS ARE MEMORIZING THE SETTINGS OF THE PRIMARY CHORD TONES FOR EACH KEY (MUSCLE MEMORY/MOTOR CORTEX), AND ALL THE WHILE THE EARS ARE LISTENING INTENSELY (LIMBIC BRAIN AND CEREBRAL CORTEX).

Violinists now have a chance to be creative by bringing their instrument's heritage into new forms of music. The choice is either to stick to tradition or to try out new instrumental techniques. This experimentation is a risk which I do not regret having taken as it brought me a lot of excitement and success beyond my dreams.

- Jean-Luc Ponty

Five Approaches To Improvisation

There are at least five major approaches to improvisation, and if you cultivate each of them, you will be able to create interesting and even powerful solos.

Choose a style and tune in this book and use the appropriate accompaniment on practice CD to apply each of the following steps:

1) Melodic Improvisation

Focusing your ears totally on the melody, weave a line that embellishes upon and harmonizes with the melody. To develop this approach, memorize the melody first. To test your knowledge of the melody, play it against a metronome or accompaniment and drop out at random points in the melody, coming back in wherever it's moved ahead to. Challenge yourself by varying the lengths of time you play and drop out.

Then try to weave an improvisation around the melody. If you can't hear the melody in your inner ear, stop playing and wait until you can. This is like edging out onto a limb. Go a little at a time until you can play more and more complex versions of the melody (using ornamentation and harmonization) without losing track of it in your inner ear.

2) Tonal Center

The chord changes to many pieces can often be ignored and the soloist can base their improvisation on one key using one scale. The key signature is usually the best clue as to the scale, but you must inspect the melody to be certain. Sometimes the tune can be in a minor key, or use a modal scale (see **Modes**).

You may be wondering at this point how it is possible to homogenize an entire tune into one scale. The key to understanding this in full, is through understanding how chord forms alter scales. As you study the chord/scale section of this chapter, you will see that each chord symbol instructs the player to lower or raise particular notes in the key. When this occurs, you are often inadvertently using the same notes as a major or minor scale in another key; the tonal center and chord tones are different, but the scale tones are the same.

For instance, if you flat the seventh of any key, it will share the same scale tones as a major scale located a fifth below. (Example: a G7 chord symbol tells you to lower the seventh of G major. Since that key only had one sharp to begin with, it is left with no sharps or flats. It now shares the same scale tones as C major. The key of C major is located a fifth below G.)

Let's take a look at the tune Kia (on page 68) in the Irish unit as a further example. The key signature tells us that the melody is in the key of C. But on closer examination, we see that the tune keeps referring to a D. We look at the chords and we see that each measure starts with a D minor chord. The D minor scale uses the same notes as C major, but from D to D.

At this point, you might be saying "Why bother having chord changes if you only end up using the same scale to improvise on for the whole piece anyway?" It's the chord changes that bring harmonic motion into the piece. If you only had one chord for accompaniment, there would be little color or interest to the piece.

3) Tonal Center With Lead Tones

As you build your improvisation around the tonal center of the tune, listen for moments when a note in the scale asks to be raised or lowered a half step, before returning to the scale. These "lead tones" are actually notes that come from the chord changes; if you listen carefully enough, you can hear them begging to be played! You don't need to know the chord changes to do this, and it's actually a wonderful ear training exercise.

For instance, your ears may insist on guiding you to flat the second tone of the A minor scale (by playing a Bb) in the second measure of the tune. You don't need to know that there is a Bb7 chord being used in the accompaniment to be able to make use of it within your improvisation. Or later, you may feel the urge to raise the seventh tone of the A minor scale; once again, your ears can lead you to that G# long before you understand that it is the major third of an E7 chord.

4) Chord Changes

In folk, Latin, blues and jazz, the key signature only applies to the melody. Once you start to improvise, you can build your lines out of the chord symbols to create a more sophisticated solo than one based on a single scale. Each chord symbol tells you what key to play in, what type of scale to use, and for how long. You will need to learn the primary chord tones (1 3 5 7) and scales of the chords in the piece. (See Chords on page 39)

Think of each chord change like a coded road map; each will guide your ears and left hand into in a new tonal center. The chord tones of a piece are important to emphasize while improvising; they are the pillars of the improvisation. The other notes of the scale are vehicles to carry you to and away from the chord tones in new and interesting ways.

When learning a tune, review the chords and scales carefully to gain command of each scale and its primary chord tones so that they are fully available to you while improvising. Pick a tune from the styles section and after learning the melody, review the chord and scale tones of the piece. Then build an improvisation in which you focus primarily upon bringing the chord tones out in varying order, using scale tones like staircases that lead you in and out of the chord tones.

Once you become more adept at this, try not to jump to the root note of each key as the chord appears, but rather attempt to "thread" your way from chord to chord.

5) A Consortium of All Four

As you become stronger at effectively using each of the four approaches to improvisation outlined above, you will experience a natural integration of the acuity of your listening with your technique and knowledge of theory. This creates a multi-dimensional use of your mental resources while improvising.

Hybrid Scales

It would be boring if every tune you played relied on only one chord, so just about every tune you come across will use various chords in its accompaniment to spice it up. The choice of instruments, as well as how they're used rhythmically to play those chords will help shape the style. You can always rely on the key signature (which will tell you how to place your fingers across the four strings) to get you started, and rely on your ears to guide you as you improvise.

The more you know about key signatures and chords, the less chance there will be that you slip and slide around searching for appropriate pitches as you invent lines to play.

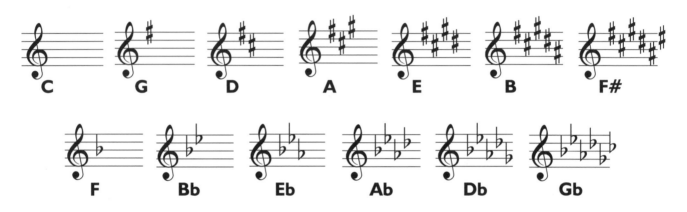

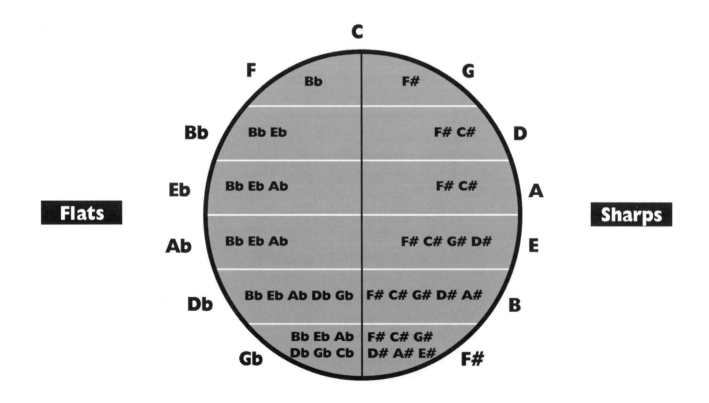

In the previous chapter, we discussed the use of a tonal center or chords tones for improvisation. In many instances, there is another option available to us as well. We can create a hybrid scale that takes the best of what two or three chords have to offer. Now we are no longer only using the scale from the key signature, or confining ourselves to the tonal guidelines of each chord. We have selected a group of notes that can work all of the way across the tune.

For instance, here are the chords to a Latin montuno and the hybrid scale that can be used to solo across them:

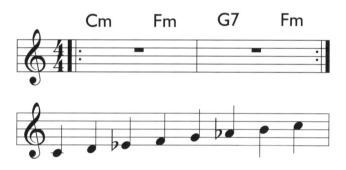

Notice how the same seven notes can be used regardless of whether you start on the C, F, or G as the tonal center.

If you are unable to figure out the hybrid scale by ear, then there are certain guidelines you can use to help determine which set of notes will work best over a series of chords.

The 2nd, 4th, and 6th tones of the scale are often called "avoid notes" (except in country and bluegrass, which love 6ths) because they clash with the chord tones when dwelled upon. They are better used as passing tones to carry us to the chord tones. We can sometimes alter the 2nd and 6th tones by flatting them (depending upon the style).

In jazz we also have the option of raising the 4th tone of the key, which we just did to the montuno's F scale to help it conform to the hybrid scale.

In some contexts we can also raise the 7th in a minor scale, which we just did to the G7 scale in the montuno sequence outlined above. It works because it acts as a lead tone back to the tonic.

Which notes do we alter and when? This is based upon the context as well as what our ears tell us.

For instance, a raised 4th can give a very modern sound. A flatted second can sound extremely ethnic. A flat 6 can help a minor scale blend into its surrounding chords more fluidly.

Experiment for yourself to decide.

Rhythm Violin

Most people think of the violin as a melodic or soloistic instrument, but there's a lot that it can contribute to create a rhythmic backdrop while other musicians are soloing. Whether it's using a repetitive rhythm on a single tone or double-stop, or making a textured backdrop by utilizing the bow differently, you can create some interesting accompaniments.

If you want to form double-stops, you can combine any two notes from the chord's primary tones: 1 3 5. Just remember to flat or sharp the chord tones in accordance with the chord symbols. Use the section **The Chords** at the end of this chapter for more information on chord forms.

Experiment by tempering classical techniques like tremolo (a short fast bow at the tip) spiccato (bounced bow) with bluegrass techniques, like the "chop technique," developed extensively by Richard Greene and Turtle Island String Quartet. In this technique, the bow creates a pitched percussive noise by using gravity to drop the bow at the frog, hitting the string in a rhythmic fashion.

You can view Green's video "Bluegrass Fiddle" (See **References**) to learn more about the chop technique.

Here are a few suggested rhythms for you to try against **Track Two** of the practice CD.

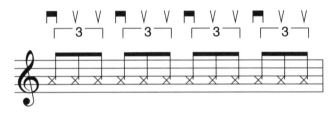

Let's try taking a simple musical phrase you might encounter when playing backup for a vocalist, and explore a few rhythmic phrases you might use against it

Modal Settings

How pitch space is "cut up" or divided octave to octave, is mostly a cultural affair. Throughout history there have been disagreements as to how many pitches define an octave. While the Western scale has eight notes, and twelve possible keys, scales with twenty-two steps were used in India in the fifth century A.D., and the Middle East has scales ranging from 17 tones up to 53! Their tuning systems include quarter tones and even smaller intervals that Western ears aren't able to identify with the same specificity.

There are many cultures that place each piece of music in a specific key, using a specific type of scale for the entire improvisation. For instance, in India each melody is based on a specific type of scale, called a raga, and the raga's scale is then used for improvisation once the melody has been stated. For instance, here is a scale that can be found in India:

The term "mode" describes the use of seven tones or pitches moving in a diatonic (scale-like) fashion octave to octave. There are a number of folk tunes that we call "modal." In this case we usually mean tunes that use a flat seventh in their scale or are minor. But whether it is called a *Maqam* (an Arabic term for mode), a *Makam* (Turkish), a *Mugam* (Azerbaijani), or a *Dastgah* (Iranian and Persian), the musicians will use that group of notes as the basis for their improvisation.

Mixolydian

Dorian minor

Natural minor

Melodic minor

Harmonic minor

In jazz we use the term "modes" to describe the seven scales adopted from Ancient Greece. The use of modes in jazz compositions became popular in the fifties and shifted attention from melody-based or chord-based improvisation to scale-based.

To create a successful improvisation using a mode (scale), you must familiarize yourself

Ionian

Dorian

b3   b7

Phrygian

b2   b3   b6   b7

Lydian

#4

Mixolydian

b7

Aeolian

b3   b6   b7

Locrian

b2   b3   b5   b6   b7

A DRONE IS A CONTINUOUSLY HELD PITCH THAT CAN BE USED AS A BACKDROP FOR IMPROVISATION. THE IMPROVISATION CAN UTILIZE ANY TYPE OF SCALE IN THAT KEY.

with its notes as thoroughly as possible (see my book *Improvising Violin* for the use of patterns for mastering scales). Practicing the scale tones is a start, but keep in mind the fact that when you set out to build an improvisation on those scale tones, you aren't going to want to run up and down in consecutive order. Get a sense of finger position so that you have a mental map of where the first finger will be placed across the four strings in that key, the second finger, the third, and then the fourth.

You can also prepare yourself for improvisation by practicing jumping into the key on any of your four strings, and moving diatonically (scale-wise) as well as moving intervalically to any note within the scale, whether it's a small step (an interval like a second or third) or a large leap (a fourth, or even a ninth). If you are the kind of player who detests practicing scales and patterns, you can start each practice session with a free improvisation on the scale of your choice, staying with it until you can move freely and cleanly within the key.

Create an improvisation in the key of D using the drone on the practice CD.

Track Three

♪ - try to avoid referring to or resolving on the tonic (the key's root) until the end

♪ - experiment using some of the modal scales outlined here or invent your own

♪ - try teaming up with a friend or student, and take turns holding a drone while the other improvises over it using a mode

The Cycle

Imagine that I could provide you with a magic formula that would give you at least 75% of the skills you might need to play blues, swing, and jazz, and to play these styles well.

I can!

Master the exercises on the following three pages and you will shock yourself at what you will be able to do.

Why are these exercises so potent? Well, we've taken the most popular chord in all of blues, swing, and jazz (the dominant seventh chord, which uses a major third, a perfect fifth, and a flatted seventh), the most popular harmonic movement in these styles (moving through the keys down in fifths or up in fourths -- same difference) and worked through the twelve keys until you are certain that you have the information in your auditory memory (your ears), your muscle memory (your hands), your right brain (mental maps of the space relationships between the notes), and your left brain (verbal, analytical, linear mental processing that enables you to name where you are and identify sequence relationships).

When we improvise we need to have total mastery over each key presented in the piece. This means that you must be able to come in at any point in the key, (not just the root) and move anywhere from there seamlessly, while adding appropriate stylistic ornamentation or substitutions (notes that can be used in place of others that create a more jazz-like sound).

Root Notes

Using the practice CD, start by playing just the root notes of the twelve keys. The accompaniment will give you eight beats per key. You can move down in fifths or up in fourths. Either will navigate you through the correct series of pitches.

Please note that the following examples have not been written out in all twelve keys. This is to prevent you from standing at your music stand and reading. You will not benefit from these exercises unless you are thinking your way through as well as listening fully. It will require harder work, and yield greater results! Make sure you move through all twelve keys of the cycle on each of the following exercises:

First octave: bottoms up

Play the root and third of each key only when you are familiar with the progression, and know where you are at all times.

Then play the root, third, and the fifth, and finally add the flatted seventh, moving through all twelve keys in each case.

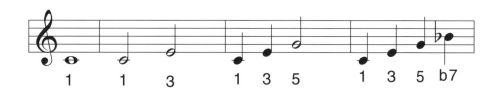

1   1   3   1   3   5   1   3   5   b7

First octave: tops down

Now play through the cycle from the third of each key down to its root. Then start on the fifth of each key, moving through its major third down to the root. Once that is

stable, start on the flat seventh of each key, moving down through its chord tones until you reach the root.

Second octave: bottoms up

1   3   1   3   5   1   3   5   b7

Second octave: tops down

3   1   5   3   1   b7   5   3   1

Two octaves up

In the keys of Db through F#, coordinate your fingerings so that you always play your last two notes on top with your second and fourth fingers.

Two octaves down

Start on the seventh of each key with your pinky. This exercise will strengthen your ability to hit a high note cleanly without the preparation that comes by walking your way up. You will also have an opportunity to strengthen your pinky action. To get the most out of this exercise, make sure you land on the tip of your pinky, not the pad, and try to hear the pitch in your inner ear before you land on it.

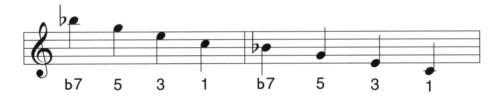

Loops Up

Now put your four chord tones to use in this looped pattern. Here is an opportunity to practice slurring smoothly across string crossings.

Loops Down

Inversions

Since you don't always want to start a musical phrase on the root of the chord, it's useful to practice coming in on the third of the key (called first inversion), the fifth (second inversion), and the seventh (third inversion). Place the rest of the chord tones on top.

Zig Zag

When improvising over chord changes, the hand must make fluidly incremental moves up and down the fingerboard, often jumping from flat keys to sharp keys in a split second. This next exercise will help you build the necessary technique for that action. In this pattern, you will be playing from the third down to the root (notice that we are now incorporating scale tones), the fifth down to the third, and then the seventh down to the fifth in both octaves. Try challenging yourself further, by never crossing strings in the midst of a three-or four-note figure. This will give you practice in second and fourth positions. Relax and float your hand up and down.

Chromatic Passing Tones

Here are six types of embellishments that you can use within your improvisation. Choose one ornament and add it to each root note in the cycle; then to the root and third of each key; root, third, and fifth; and finally to the root, third, fifth, and dominant seventh. Then you can repeat this exercise using each of the other ornaments illustrated below.

Substituting the Fourth for the Third

To develop a more modern sound, you can substitute the fourth tone of the key for the third tone. This note can also be thought of as the eleventh of the key.

Raising the Fourth: Lydian Dominant

When we lower the seventh, it is called a dominant seventh chord. Raising the fourth is called lydian (see the modes). A lydian dominant scale can be superimposed over any dominant seventh chord to create a more interesting sound while soloing.

If you raise the fourth tone of the scale and place it above the octave, you are using an extension called a sharp eleven. Within the octave, this sharp four could be heard as a flat five, and therefore not bring anything

terribly different to jazz harmony, since the flat five had already been popularized by the blues in the twenties, and repopularized by bebop in the fifties. In the blues, swing, bluegrass, and even country music, the flat five is used to lead up to the fifth tone of the key. But used and heard as a sharp four, it is called a tritone, because it cuts the octave exactly in two equal halves; placed above the octave, it becomes an extension.

Working the Sixth

The sixth tone of the scale is a bit finicky. It doesn't always sound good if you dwell on it, unless the rhythm section is using a major or minor sixth chord (1 3 5 6 or 1 b3 5 6), which is quite popular in country music. But you will need to be certain of where the 6th is in relationship to the tonic of each key in

order to know whether or not you want to bring it out or avoid it. Here's a little phrase I nabbed from a solo by jazz violinist Claude "Fiddler" Williams. The line starts on the seventh of the key, moves through the chord tones and resolves on the sixth. Try moving it through the cycle.

Working the Extensions: the ninth

Who are we kidding? The ninth is the same note as the second tone in the scale. Why bother practicing it? It may not sound like much when it's used as a scale tone in the first octave, but when you add it on top of a seventh chord, it's delicious. This line starts on the third of each key and moves up through the ninth.

Working the Extensions: the eleventh

You guessed it! The eleventh is the same note as the fourth. In jazz and swing, when you raise it, it can sound a lot more interesting than leaving it alone. This pattern starts on the third of the key, moves up through the dominant seventh and the ninth to the sharp eleventh, and resolves back down to the third of the key.

Working the Extensions: the thirteenth

The thirteen is the same note as the sixth. Again, when added into the second octave, it adds a jazzy sound. In this pattern, we are again starting on the third, moving up through the ninth and eleventh, reaching the thirteenth and using a chromatic passing tone to resolve on the fifth of each key in the cycle.

Double Stops

Almost every style covered in this book can benefit from the use of double stops. The folk styles tend to benefit most from droning the melody against open strings:

Unisons sound great (fingered E note against open E string, or A against A, or D against D, depending upon what key you're in); as well as various combinations of the root, third, and fifth of the chord.

Blues, jazz, and Latin really zip when you add the flatted seventh into the equation and Flamenco sounds fantastic with octaves.

When practicing double-stops, tune the lower note first, roll the bow into the upper pitch, and then "cream" them together. Keep in mind that a good bowed chord comes from positioning the height of the right elbow so that the bow rides easily on both strings. Don't use pressure or you will end up overworking and sounding scratchy!

I like to prepare my facility with double-stops by practicing them slowly, moving through each key in the piece of music I'm working on, exploring every possible combination of the primary chord tones (root, third, fifth, and sixth or seventh, depending upon the style; flatting or raising chord tones according to the chord symbols) across each set of strings: G/D, D/A, and A/E.

On page 37, you will find a chart of double-stops in all twelve keys. In all cases, the pitches I've combined to create the chords consist of either the root, the third, or the fifth of the key. To work with the sixth or the seventh is easy. You will find the seventh a half degree below the octave if it is a major chord, or a whole degree below the octave if it is a minor or dominant seventh chord. The sixth is a whole step above the fifth of the key. To find the fifth, just bring your finger straight across from the root. Since the violin is tuned in fifths, we can always find the fifth of the key by using the same finger on the next parallel string up.

W hat's the difference between a violin and a fiddle? It's a fiddle if you're buying it, it's a violin if you're selling it!

On the following six pages you will find the seven basic chord types represented in all twelve keys. Use this section as a reference when working on any tune that presents chords or keys that are unfamiliar to you. Learn the chord tones first, and then the accompanying chordal scale.

The Chords .

I have provided you with chord reference charts on the following pages. If you have never worked with chords before, this can look quite overwhelming. Try thinking like an architect and plan a course of action over a preferred period of time. Then do a little bit at a time each day rather than post-poning and postponing until you're out of time!

> A MINOR THIRD IS BUILT OF ONE WHOLE STEP AND ONE HALF STEP. A MAJOR THIRD IS BUILT OF TWO WHOLE STEPS. EVERY CHORD IS A SEQUENCE OF MINOR AND MAJOR THIRDS STACKED ON TOP OF EACH OTHER. YOU JUST HAVE TO LEARN THE ORDER FOR EACH CHORD TYPE.

When taking consistent action, I have seen players learn these seven basic chord types in all twelve keys in anywhere from one month to three years.

All Western music is built on thirds and once you catch on to the sound of minor and major thirds, the increment of space on the fingerboard between each, and the names of the notes, you are well on your way to learning about all of the chords outlined here. They're all built on minor and major thirds.

Here are three suggested approaches to working with chords:

1) Tackle one tune at a time, playing the root notes of the chords; then the root and third; the root, third, and fifth; and finally the root, third, fifth, and seventh. Use the following charts if you aren't sure about how to configure each chord.

2) Begin to familiarize yourself with the keys that you come across the most often in the styles you enjoy the most. Most fiddle tunes share a preference for the keys of G, D, A, and E, and tend to use mostly major, minor, and dominant seventh chords.

3) Focus on the cycle exercises to master moving through the twelve keys (or limit yourself to a smaller group of keys) and then gradually incorporate the other chord types into your work.

Δ *or* M *or* Maj means "major"	= 1 2 **3** 4 **5** 6 **7**
7 *or* dom7 means "dominant seventh"	= 1 2 **3** 4 **5** 6 **b7**
- *or* -7 *or* min7 means "minor seventh"	= 1 2 **b3** 4 **5** 6 **b7**
mMaj means "minor major"	= 1 2 **b3** 4 **5** 6 **7**
o *or* dim means "diminished"	= 1 2 **b3** 4 **b5** b6 **bb 7** 7
∅ *or* m7b5 means "half diminished"	= 1 b2 **b3** 4 **b5** b6 **b7**
7+9 *or* alt means "altered"	= 1 b9 #9 **3** #4 **#5** **b7**

NOTE: While blues and jazz love the seventh of the key, in folk/country tunes you can often avoid using it altogether. It tends to sound too dissonant.

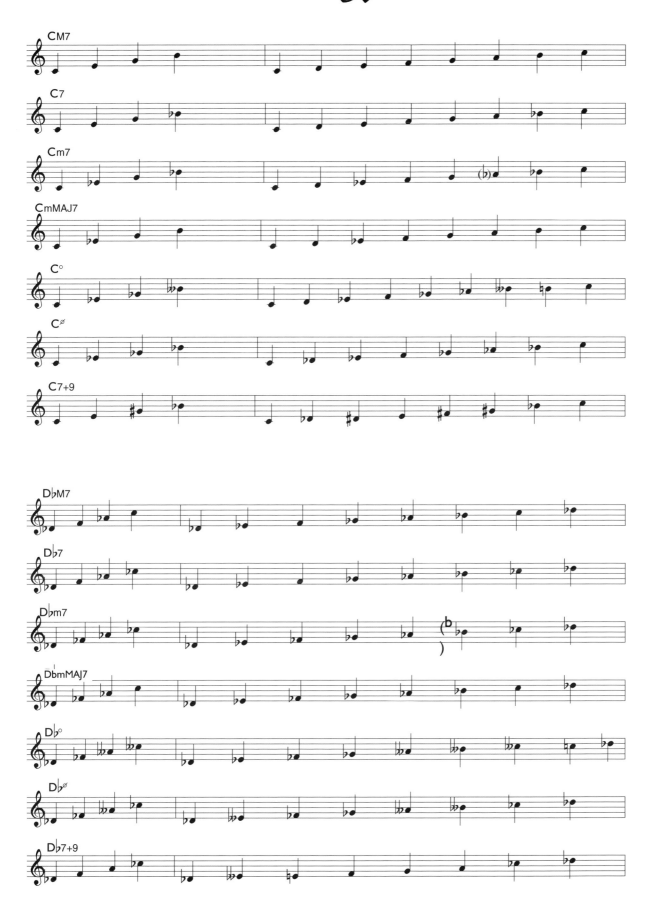

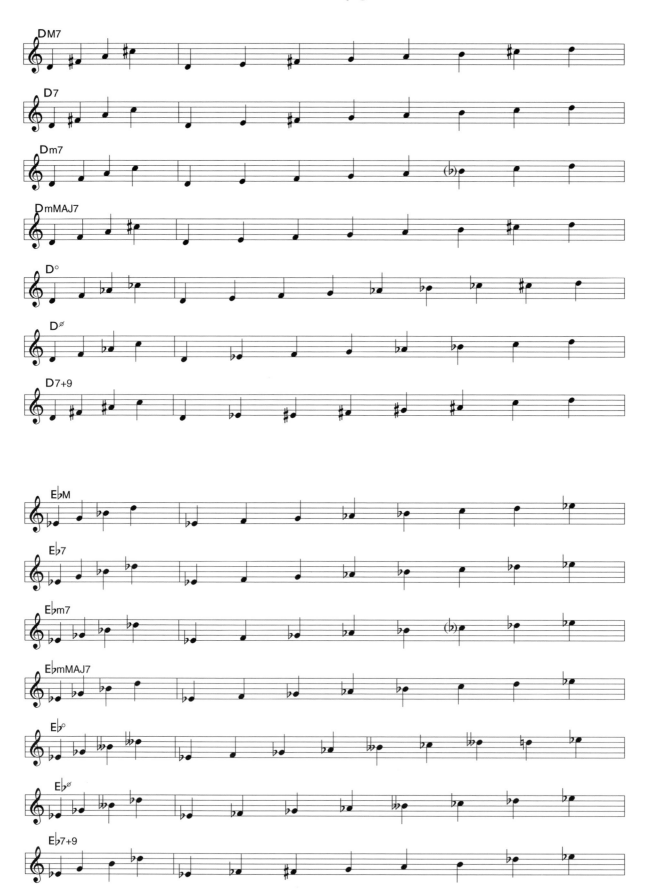

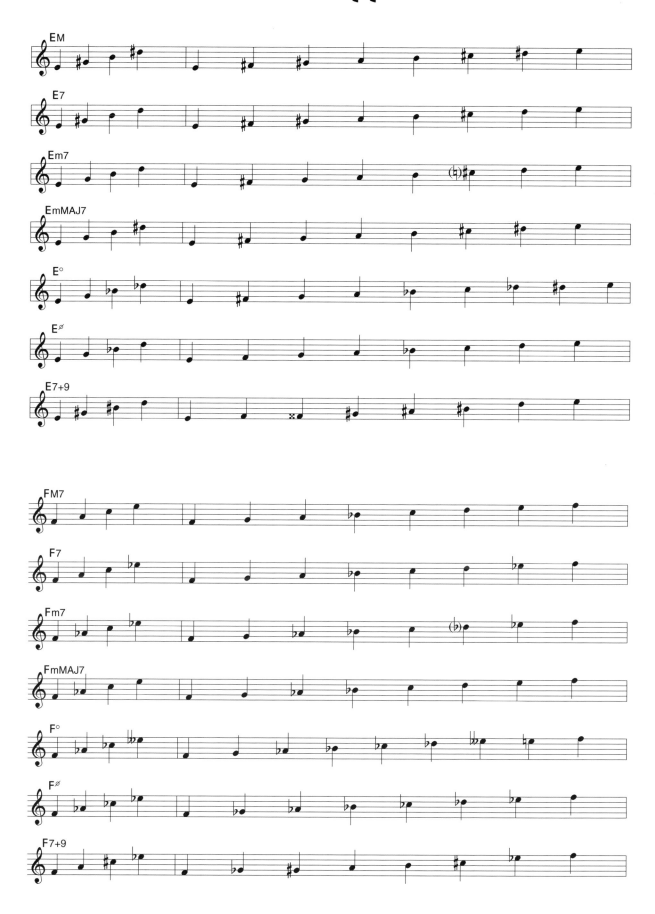

- 43 -

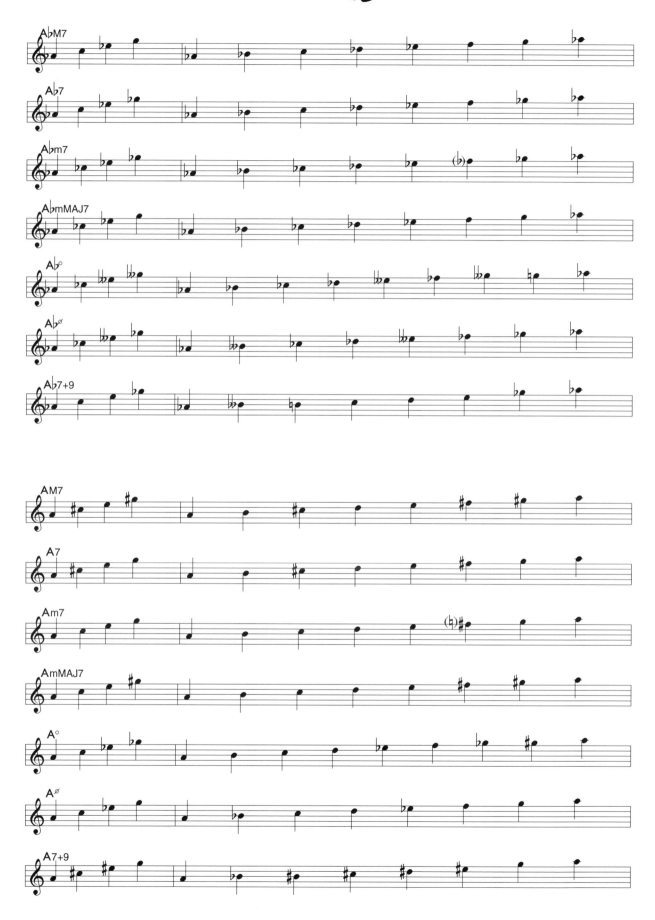

- **44** -

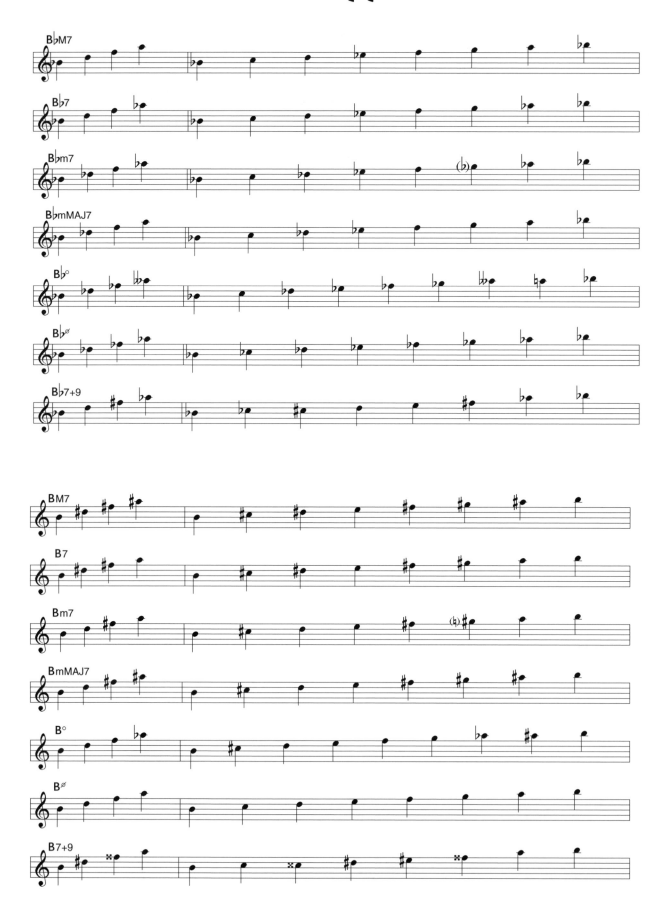

The Styles

The Basics

As we become immersed in the style section of this book, I want to be very clear with you that my intention here is teaching you how to improvise. Therefore we will be examining the bowings and left-hand techniques, as well as structures and harmonic devices of each style to create new approaches to improvisation. If, in your journey through these styles, you find one that particularly appeals to you, you can immerse yourself in that tradition by listening to as many traditional artists in that genre as possible, and taking lessons with a teacher who specializes in the style.

Back in 1972, after a decade of classical training, I ordered my first book of fiddle tunes through the mail. I ran to greet the postman every day for weeks in anticipation of busting loose and turning myself into a fiddler on the spot. That book was to be my salvation because I longed to experience something new on my violin.

The book finally arrived. I had been conditioned through classical training to think that all music could be communicated through written notation. I placed it on my music stand, played through every tune on every page, and threw the book down on the floor in utter disgust. "This just sounds like short classical tunes!"

It took me a number of years to realize that non-classical styles don't communicate their essence visually. Fiddle styles, blues, swing, jazz, are all languages that are better learned by ear. When notated, they tell you little or nothing about how to create their unique sound. Most tunes are written without bowings or ornamentation, because it slows the reader down. The writer usually assumes that you will know what to do to make that tune sound appropriately traditional. I have done the best I can with text, notation, and practice tracks to give you as much information as I can to get you started in each style. The reference section at the end of the book provides important resources for each style. It is by no means a complete listing, but will supply you with some core listening and reading materials in each style to help supplement your learning process.

When having trouble playing a given tune, whether with physical coordination, phrasing, memorization, or giving effective mental direction to hand movement, I've discovered that the use of "site-specific" exercises are most beneficial in facilitating immediate improvement.

You will find preparatory exercises offered in each unit to help get you ready for the challenges specific to that style. These warm-ups have been designed to help you isolate and master the types of challenges that come up in non-classical repertoire. They're based on the idea that when you are playing a tune you should be free to focus on the melody or the improvisation. Therefore, if you choose a warm-up that fully prepares you technically and stylistically, then your mind and body will be much more cooperative when you move on to playing the tune or improvising in that style.

Let's look at some general technical and musical issues common to all players before we start on the specifics of each style.

Supporting the Instrument

Many fiddlers tend to hold their instrument slightly in front of them on their chest, rather than on the shoulder. This is a leftover from the days when most fiddlers called off square dances and needed their voice-box free to speak and sing. Another contributing factor was the lack of resources when it came to different types of chinrests and shoulder rests.

Times have changed: protect yourself. We haven't just come in from a day's labor out on the field. Many of us spend the day seated at a desk, or working at a physical job that requires repetitive motion rather than an old-fashioned complete work-out of the whole body. This makes it harder for our muscles to manage distorted body positions.

Holding the instrument low locks the left elbow into one position and forces the hand to operate at a difficult angle, reducing the forearm's ability to rotate and line the fingers up perpendicular to the fingerboard. It also forces the bowing arm too far back by the right side, unnecessarily engaging the right shoulder and wrist during string crossings. Use a shoulder rest to free the left hand from the responsibility of holding up the fiddle, and to help increase mobility in the left arm. Choose the most comfortable shoulder rest for your body-type by visiting a string shop and trying out their various models.

Using a shoulder rest and chinrest that suit your body-type will protect you from having to lift your left shoulder or clamp down with your chin to hold the instrument. Make sure that the chinrest fits the width and length of your chin. Turn your head halfway to the left and slightly lower your chin. The instrument should be right there, waiting for you, without having to contort your body!

My two favorite shoulder rests are the "Kun," which is best for medium to wide shoulder span; or "Wolf Forte Primo" for narrow shoulders or a slight build. Make sure that the screw that attaches the feet on the side of the violin that sits over your chest is screwed further in than the one above your shoulder to tilt the face of the fiddle towards your bow arm.

Remember that everyone has a different body-type, and it's best to try a few models out before making a final decision. Base your decision on a feeling of comfort and security without strain.

Bow Length

Many players equate speed with effort and inadvertently use too much bow length, particularly while playing fast. Others have been taught to move the bow in long strides for classical literature. Since the only way to get a quality sound when using too much bow length is to move the bow out towards the fingerboard, this offense can be easily detected by the amount of rosin you will find on or near the fingerboard.

As you speed up, use less hair, center the bow between the bridge and the fingerboard, relax more, and try to use the downbow on each string crossing as an opportunity to release your arm weight into gravity, thereby giving your muscles constant relief rather than constant contraction (tension), which can impair fluid motion.

The biceps muscle is its strongest when your arm is at a right angle, so this is the preferred arm position for fast, repetitive bowing.

Crossing Strings

Some players try to initiate fast movement from the wrist. The wrist muscle is extremely weak compared to the forearm; this makes detailed control much more difficult and can cause injuries such as carpal tunnel syndrome or tendinitis later.

I use two terms to describe the primary movement of the upper arm during string crossings: pump or pivot. While the note-to-note movement should be a push/pull motion powered by the forearm (and the biceps muscle), the upper arm acts like a pump, raising and lowering your arm to move you from string to string.

If you're bobbing between the same two strings for an entire passage, though, you would do better to place your upper arm so that your bow is resting on both strings, keep your upper arm fairly still, and pivot your forearm from the elbow for the repetitive string crossing. Practice isolating each movement using short repetitive bows to develop control. But whatever you do, don't allow your upper arm to move forward and back on short bows. It will look like you're sawing a piece of wood, and sound about the same!

Flailing

The further away you lift your left hand's fingers from the fingerboard when not using them, the further you'll have to travel back to place them down on time and in tune. Economy of motion will bring effortless speed and teamwork in the left hand. Eliminate all unnecessary finger motion by hovering close to the fingerboard all of the time.

Uneven Rhythm

Many players tend to speed up on the easier passages and slow down on the difficult ones without being aware of it. Unfortunately, this becomes a habit. Try using a metronome at a slow speed to even everything out, and then gradually (notch by notch) increase the speed. If you start to play out of tune or tense up on certain passages, come back a notch or two until your movement is fluid and tone and pitch are restored.

Effort Versus Release

For speed or right-hand embellishment, use economy of motion and a light touch. If you hover the fingers of your left hand over the fingerboard, rather than letting them fly away in between notes, and use just enough pressure to get a clear tone, and no more, you will be able to create a fluid, easy-going technique. Basically, if your fingers feel stiff after practice, you're pressing too hard.

It's easier on your muscles to move your fingers with a light touch rather than hammering your fingertips down for embellishment or fast motion in the left hand, and the more you use arm weight to create tone on the right side, (rather than muscular pressure), the more success you'll have when you increase the tempo, particularly if you maintain a light bow hold rather than pinching with your thumb. So don't squeeze the bow! I should be able to pull the bow out of your hand easily, even when you're playing loudly and passionately.

Strings

My favorite strings are the Helicore (medium) by D'Addario. They are smooth to the touch for slides, give a fast response, and break in quickly. I change my set of strings every six months to avoid playing on dull or false strings. When strings get too old, they lose their consistency and can be harder on the player when it comes to accurate pitch or a good sound.

Some fiddlers like to use steel strings because they don't go out of tune and last a long time. But I still maintain that they need to be changed, because the resiliency of the sound wears out after a while. Steel does last longer (8 to 10 months), but they're thinner and can be harder on the fingertips if you're not used to them.

Bows and Fiddles

The sound of the instrument and how it feels in your hands should be placed above "pedigree." Don't allow information like who made the violin, and how famous a reputation they have affect your decision to buy, unless you are a collector and only like to own instruments that have market value.

Make sure that all cracks on the face of the instrument have been glued, and that the seams aren't open. Close one eye and look down the fingerboard to make sure it isn't warped, and look at the bridge from above to make sure it is straight. The curve of the bridge should match the exact curve of the fingerboard so that both hands transit across an identical arch.

If the strings look suspiciously high off the fingerboard and are hard to press down, have their distance measured to make sure that there isn't a problem.

When you try out bows, choose one that creates a great tone on your violin (they all sound different). Then make sure that the center of the stick doesn't easily flop down to the string while you are playing. That indicates a weak stick. If you feel like you

have to work really hard to get the bow to move, then it may have a sluggish response rate. Shopping for a new bow, I always look for a nice, warm tone, and a responsive feel.

For a composite bow, I recommend the carbon fiber bow, Musicary, sold by SHAR catalogue. It comes in five colors and is a bargain. My blue Musicary bow equals my best wood bow in tone and response!

Repair

It's common to need to have the seams glued from time to time when the instrument is exposed to excessive humidity or dryness. The bridge can warp over the years, so it's good to have it replaced every decade or so. Keep an eye open for new cracks so that you can catch them early before they spread. Then head for your local repairperson.

Instrument Care

Wipe the rosin off the strings and the face of the instrument at the end of the day, when you are putting your fiddle away. If you like to leave the instrument out all of the time, cover its face with a towel or piece of cloth. Dust can get inside, and old rosin can melt and destroy the varnish. Remember that someone might have spent the better part of a year of their life making this piece of art so that you could make music every day!

Tuners on the Tailpiece

I recommend a tailpiece with the four fine-tuners built into it, particularly if you're planning to amplify your instrument. Fine-tuners will enable you to make faster pitch adjustments to the strings with less trauma to your left hand and ears -- particularly if you don't have a fancy fiddle with pegs that turn with perfect ease. Four "E" fine tuners added to a tailpiece just won't do the job (unless you have steel strings), because those tuners were only designed to handle the thin E string.

Amplification

There are many choices now available for amplification, ranging from amplified a-coustic to solid-body violins. Here are some of my personal favorites:

The L.R. Baggs is an excellent pickup system. It can be used on a trashy fiddle as long as you purchase the Baggs preamp to modify the tone to one you like. You will need a repairman to install it, because it arrives built into a bridge that has to be carved to fit your instrument. Use of this system will alter the natural acoustic sound of the instrument.

The Kurmann soundpost system provides an excellent amplified acoustic sound and can be mounted inside of a fine instrument without ruining the bridge or altering the acoustic sound of the violin. The system comes already mounted inside of the soundpost and must be fit by a repairman.

The Yamaha Silent Violin is an excellent economical choice for players who need to practice quietly, for use in hotel rooms, and for no-frills amplification (it doesn't rate highly in tone-production).

There are also many fine solid-body violins by Zeta, Mark Wood, Tucker Barrett, and others. Consult my book, *Improvising Violin*, for additional information, or look through the ads of STRINGS Magazine.

Protecting your Ears

Jean-Luc Ponty kindly sent me an E-mail close to the completion of this book, asking me to warn players of the potential damage to their ears when using amplification and/or playing in loud bands.

During rehearsals, try to keep volume settings as low as possible. If surrounded by loud instruments such as percussion, brass, or musicians who already suffer from hearing loss and have to crank their amps to hear what they're doing, wear ear-plugs.

I carry ear-plugs with me wherever I go to protect my ears when riding in small airplanes, waiting for the subway, or in unusually loud restaurants. I also have specially designed ear-plugs that filter noise but give me a pure representation of pitch and tone while playing the violin, in case I have to work in a noisy environment.

Somewhere in the funny/strange, funny/sad annals of bad blues jams in New York City, amid the one-armed harp players, and the Japanese Stevie Ray Vaughn clones who sing "Flooding Down in Texas" phonetically, mention must be made of a certain Jimi Hendrix impersonator (new in town from Alabama) who put his hand in his jacket and threatened to pull a gun on the other jammers when they balked at playing "Voodoo Chile." Perhaps the most grotesque true story involves a rather well-known New York blues personality who expressed displeasure with a fellow musician by defecating into his saxophone.

- Susan Ruel

Practice Tracks

It's tremendously important to practice improvisation with accompaniment, but many of us don't have access to ongoing jam sessions. While this book comes with practice tracks, there are many tunes and styles you will work on in the coming years that will be absorbed much more quickly through the use of a "backup band" during practice.

There are two great resources for practice tracks. Jazz Aids by Jamey Aebersold offers CDs with pre-recorded accompaniments for blues and jazz-oriented exercises and repertoire. He also offers a couple of Latin-oriented CDs.

Band in a Box by PG Music is an excellent resource if you have a computer. It is a software program that enables you to create your own accompaniments. You can choose from their wide menu of styles, control the length of the accompaniment, the speed, the chords, the key, and even get it to loop over small problematical spots in the chord changes. All you need is a computer, a midi-box, and a sound system (or computer speakers) to use this software. It's well worth the investment!

Jam Sessions

There was a great discussion on the internet in the newsgroup "FiddleL" about jam session etiquette. It made me realize that this is a subject that's very important, yet seldom discussed. It's just expected that when an individual arrives at a group session for the first time, they'll know how to fit in without any prior information. Often, this is not true!

Each tradition has formed its own "jam session procedures" when it comes to group sessions. Not all of these traditions embrace improvisation. If you're looking for an opportunity to improvise in traditional styles, you may have to create some of your own sessions where the musicians arrive prepared to do things in a new way.

Before getting started, it's well worth making a few agreements on how you want to proceed, so that there aren't any misunderstandings and therefore bad feelings created. For instance, you will need to address agreements about the length of the solos, who chooses the tunes, setting the tempo so that it's in everyone's reach, bringing the volume down for vocals or unamplified violin, and so on.

> Most of us learn the hard way. It took me a while to realize that different genres of music have different jamming rules. It's pretty obvious that if someone is singing, melody players should either stop playing, play very softly, or play unobtrusive harmonies. But woe unto an old-time player who finds him/herself among bluegrassers and doesn't understand their expectations. Bluegrass types seem to want solo breaks passed around the circle on every tune.
>
> Misunderstandings can cut both ways. A mandolin player, apparently with only bluegrass jam experience, joined an old-time jam here in California recently. He played along through a couple of tunes and then said, "Hey! Why don't you guys ever give a guy a break?" He stomped off in anger, before anyone could explain.
>
> **- Dave Barton**
> **FiddleL Newsgroup**

One of the earliest experiences I had at a jam was back in the late 60s/early 70s. I was new to improvisation, and had played at a folk festival behind a singer, using pre-arranged lines. Afterwards, there was a party at someone's house, and I wandered around until I found a cluster of musicians in the kitchen playing a tune that sounded within my reach. I joined in with great enthusiasm, playing my heart out for the duration of the piece. I ducked out for a moment to go to the bathroom, and as I returned to the kitchen door, heard them saying "She plays pretty well, but I wish she would stop for a minute and give someone else a chance!" I felt too embarrassed to go back into the room. I won't tell you the names of the people because they became quite famous a few years after that experience. I learned an important lesson the hard way!

Everyone is eager to make music, no matter what their level is or their personality type. And a lot of people have self-esteem issues going on as to whether or not they're good enough, what others will think, and so on. But no one says anything. There's a silent drama that gets played out. Often this undercurrent makes it difficult to have the gratification that comes from making music with others.

When you arrive at a session for the first time, look around at the folks who have been coming for a while to get an idea of how people are participating before you jump in; in between tunes, you can always whisper any questions you have to whomever is hosting the event.

Some of the touchy issues that come up include 1) share the leadership; people don't like it when one person takes over; 2) if your playing skills are under par, play softly so that you don't pull the better play-ers down with you; 3) when someone is acting inappropriately, it's far kinder to give them some guidelines rather than act out behind their backs. I've heard stories of people turning the piano around or hiding chairs, and the like, just to stop someone who's irritating them from playing! 4) if someone already is playing fiddle/violin at the jam, wait until they're in between pieces and ask if it would be OK to join in, and what level of participation would be comfortable for them.

Here in Rochester, NY, we have a regular Irish jam. It's generally well-attended by fairly good musicians and a few stand-outs who really make the session run. One day, most of the stand-outs weren't there. A man with an accordion and sheet music arrived. He decided to play off the paper (not done at this session -- no one would have time to search for the music). Not the most horrible thing, since we were underpowered that night, but he proceeded to go from one tune to the next, drowning out all challengers. We were polite.

The next session he arrived with several relatives. He xeroxed his music, and handed it out. He also has a light on his music stand, as he found it too hard to read the music in the pub. His many relatives were taking videos and recordings while several more played along (with their bodhrans, of course). My friend Phil, who was here from London, said he wished he had a copy of the film they made, because he knew no one back in England would believe this guy existed. Someone must have clued our jam-buster in, because the culprit has never returned!

- Betsy Kubick

Old-Time Shuffles Along

Lightweight, easy to carry and easy to make, the fiddle was one of the first instruments brought by settlers to America. It was used to accompany dances, entertain at social gatherings, or lighten one's spirits at the end of a long hard day of work.

Celtic music in the form of Irish, Scottish, and Welsh jigs, reels, and hornpipes arrived on U.S. and Canadian soil, and evolved in many different directions, depending upon which geographic region fiddlers settled in.

When we use the term "old-time fiddle tunes," we're generally referring to *square dance tunes*, *hoedowns*, and *reels*. The ingredients that help create this style, include specific bow strokes, the use of double stops, and a strong rhythmic pulse accentuating the downbeat.

To start, you will need to familiarize yourself with some of the bowings typical of this style. These bowings can also be applied to bluegrass and even swing.

Play an A major scale (see page 56), using each of the bowings outlined here in order to help make each bowing a comfortable part of your technique:

Shuffle Stroke

Georgia Shuffle

Mixed: Shuffle and Georgia

Popular Fiddle Bowing

Popular Fiddle Bowing

The various styles of fiddling (Old-Time, Irish, Cajun, Québecois, New England, Texas, swing, etc.) are analogous to different musical languages or dialects. The best way to get started learning any style is to listen for the characteristic rhythms, accents, ornaments, tone production and sense of pitch. These qualities are more important than the tunes in defining a style. If you'd like to play Appalachian Old-Time fiddle, but you don't live in the region, get some recordings of your favorite Appalachian fiddlers and Listen, Listen, Listen. Then, Play, Play, Play. Try recording yourself and listening carefully to your playing. Then do it all Again, Again, Again and Again. The fun doesn't end, it just multiplies!

Though I could demonstrate it to some effect, I'd rather not try to write a verbal description of a Cajun shuffle versus an Old-Time shuffle, because to my ear there are so many different kinds of Cajun shuffles and Old-Time shuffles. Compare the fiddling of Kevin Wimmer and Mitch Reed, or Dewey Balfa and Canray Fontenot, or Tommy Jarrell and Ralph Blizard. It's these differences that make their music interesting and, for me, endlessly enjoyable.

Ultimately, I think that listening and developing an aural/visceral knowledge of an idiom is everything. You can no more learn a fiddle style only from a book than you can learn to speak a language purely from the printed page. Musicians involved in just one idiom may forget to take this into account, since everyone they know has a similar set of aural assumptions. When they write a musical passage for a reader already familiar with the same palette of sounds, there's a good chance that the reader will play what the writer intended. For example, imagine a traditional Irish fiddler reading a tune from O'Neil's and a classical violinist reading a Mozart minuet. Now imagine how different it might sound if they traded music.

Some fiddle traditions have long-standing written repertoires and others, such as Southern Appalachian and Cajun fiddling, have only recently been finding their way to print. But even though some Scottish, Irish and New England fiddle tunes have been in print for generations, most readers in these traditions probably use written music more to jog the memory (and preserve the tunes) than to learn the music.

So, on your journey down the road of traditional fiddling, read fiddle tunes if you find it helpful, but always remember to listen to the beautiful nuances that define each style. And most importantly, keep having fun with your fiddle!

- Jay Ungar

The double shuffle stroke adds a vibrant rhythmic pulse by crossing strings and using double-stops. Practice this bowing slowly at first, using a drop into and bounce out of gravity to keep the bow arm relaxed. Keep your hand, wrist and forearm in alignment with the tip of your elbow, and cross the strings by pumping from the elbow, lifting your upper arm up and down like a chicken! Once you are able to use this bow pattern without strain at a lively tempo on open strings, then add your left hand in.

Here's an excerpt from Orange Blossom Special that uses the double shuffle stroke:

You can see that the bow arm contributes immensely to help create this style. In fact, even the double-stops old-time is known for, are more a right-hand challenge. They usually consist of melody notes played against the drone of an open string. Many beginners mistakenly use pressure to play on the two strings simultaneously. The bow's pressure should be light. It's actually the position of the right elbow that maneuvers the bow so that you can easily glide on two strings simultaneously.

There are some double-stops that require straddling fingered notes across two strings. Start by practicing playing the bottom of the two; if you find that you are reliably in tune within the context of the melody, then pause at that spot, and roll from the lower note to the upper one, and then cream them together with that nice light bow. This process will help train both hands to coordinate properly each time the fingered double-stop comes along, enabling you to finger both notes in tune simultaneously.

To prepare for Cripple Creek, start by familiarizing yourself with the A major scale, the key the tune is based on. Make sure you can play the two-octave scale in tune, knowing the names of the notes as you play them.

Develop the shuffle stroke by playing it first on each note of the scale, then practice it on open strings, mastering playing double-stops evenly while crossing strings.

The biceps muscle moves the bow repetitively, but is at its weakest when it is lengthened. Keep your right arm at a right angle, which should place you somewhere near the center of the bow, where the natural weight of the stick can produce a good tone with the least amount of effort. This position uses the biceps muscle more efficiently.

J strongly feel that the fiddle is as much a percussion instrument as a melodic instrument and *J* treat it that way. The melodies are unique and powerful but not as complex as other styles. The most artful old-time players are the ones who can get all the characteristic rhythms and syncopation into their right hand without compromising the melody or messing up the phrasing.

You have to have listened to a tremendous amount of old-time music to play just a little bit of it. The magic in the music is what happens between the rhythm and the melody.

- Bruce Molsky

Let's work on building an old-time sound
on this tune. First, familiarize yourself with
the melody.

Cripple Creek
(bare bones melody)

Now add the shuffle stroke. When working on old-time tunes that have run-on eighths or sixteenths, you can also experiment with inserting some of the other bowings in spots where you think they will sound good.

Cripple Creek
(melody with shuffle stroke)

You can also double up on melodic figures or weave around them:

Try adding a drone. This means that you will either be hitting the open A or open E strings at all times while playing the melody. After playing the melody, base your improvisation in the key of A, incorporating double stops and shuffle stroke (or some of the other bowstrokes we've discussed) as you create lines against the accompaniment on *Track Five* of the practice CD.

Track Five

Cripple Creek
(melody with shuffle stroke and double-stops)

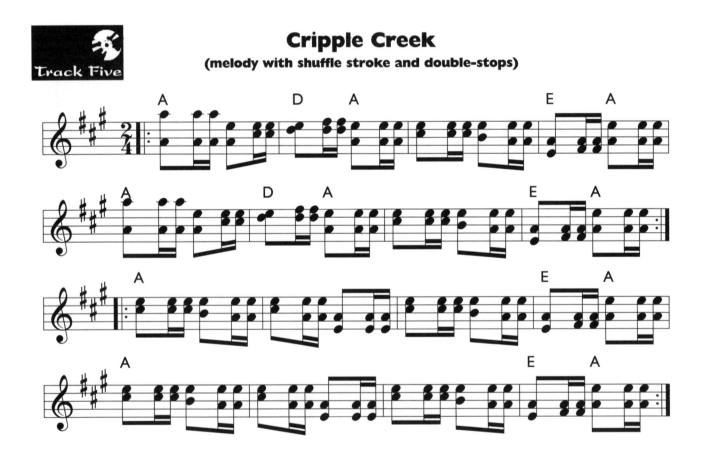

> No one feels the attraction of deep roots more than the uprooted. I will never "own" these old traditions, but they have been graciously lent to me, and I hope to return the music in as good condition as I received it.
>
> **- Sam Zygmuntowicz**

Bluegrass Frenzy

Singer and mandolinist Bill Monroe has been credited by scholars and historians as the originator of bluegrass. The vocal style, which informs the fiddle style, has a stark, mournful edge, which he would refer to as a "high, lonesome sound." Monroe openly credited the influence of Arnold Schultz, a local African-American railroad worker in Rosine, Kentucky, who was a highly talented blues fiddler as well as guitarist. He was also influenced by Appalachian ballad and church traditions.

When we think of bluegrass today, we mostly think FAST! Often the player is running sixteenth notes at 168 on the metronome. But Monroe also included spiritual songs, and solo vocals in his recordings and performances. It's his instrumental show pieces that caught on, though, and became the focal point for subsequent bluegrass bands.

Building on Texas Swing legend Bob Wills, who used two fiddles in his band, Monroe introduced a triple fiddle sound in the 1950s with his band, "The Blue Grass Boys." Some of the fiddlers that worked with him included Tex Logan, Vassar Clements, Richard Greene, Kenny Baker, Clarence "Tater" Tate, Bobby Hicks, Joe Stuart, Charlie Cline, Red Taylor, and Gordon Terry. Many of these excellent musicians went on to distinguish themselves outside of Monroe's band, making outstanding contributions to the field.

A bluegrass fiddler knows how to take the bare bones of a simple tune, and dress it up, using the slides, syncopation, and "blue notes" of the blues (b3 and b5). They also

To me, playing bluegrass is playing with Bill Monroe. To hear that mandolin chop, or that high tenor voice while fiddling, is incomparably inspiring.

Bluegrass is outcast music, it's lonesome music. The idea is to wail as hard as you can. I've heard it called "doggin it." There's a lot of black in the music; blues are paramount.

Fiddling in a bluegrass band is like picking your way through different mazes of I, IV, V harmony on top of which can lie the most inventive and unique mix of melody, blues and violinistics. The biggest challenge is to come up with classic and bluesy melodies, all different from each other, all of them profound in a bluegrass way and of course over the simplest harmony imaginable.

Bluegrass is fairly generous in how much stuff from the classical world can creep in. Really wild double and triple stops, left hand pizzicato, spiccato, harmonics, but most importantly, <u>tone</u>. The best bluegrass players play with the best tone, exactly as in the classical world. Tone and Melody are everything.

- Richard Greene

know how to double up figures, or add twists and turns to simple melodies and rhythms, all within a fiery tempo.

Refer to the units on playing the blues and old-time fiddle to develop your knowledge of fiddle bowings and slide technique.

Here are a couple of typical openings to bluegrass tunes. The bow can be landed with force, to create a staccato percussive effect. This is called the bluegrass "chop" and can create a jumping rhythmic backdrop while everyone else is soloing. The sound and coordination are best demonstrated by Richard Greene on his video, "Bluegrass Fiddle" (see References).

Another feature of this genre is the use of surprisingly dissonant and jazzy harmonies. For instance, here is an example of what two fiddles might play against each other to open a tune. Listen to some of Bill Monroe's recordings using triple fiddles to hear these wonderfully energizing harmonies.

Somewhere along the way, it became quite popular to end a bluegrass tune or bluegrass improvisation with the *Shave and a Haircut* lick; then a kind of unspoken contest emerged as to who could warp that lick so that it was still recognizable yet different. Try putting the lick into the keys of D, G, and E first, and then experiment with different ways to frame it. I've included two of a zillion possibilities. Good luck!

I intentionally chose Cripple Creek to demonstrate the bluegrass style to give you an opportunity to compare the same tune in an old-time context to what is possible in the bluegrass style. I encourage you to practice all of the bowings and the old-time version first, before dipping into this version.

Track Six

Cripple Creek
arranged by Julie Lyonn Lieberman ©1999 Huiksi Music

Country Drawl

Country music is vocal music. More often than not, the personal preferences of the singer defines the fiddle's role in the band.

Most vocalists like the lyrics to take center stage -- understandably so -- relegating the fiddle to filler lines and solos. When playing backup for a singer, it's extremely helpful to familiarize yourself with the lyrics and melody so that you can gracefully weave tasty fiddle lines in between the sung phrases.

If you're invited to play behind the singer, try to keep your lines supportive by either harmonizing with the melody, or providing simple repetitive phrases that mesh with the rhythmic values of the rest of the band. If you can't hear or understand the lyrics while you're playing, that's a sign that your lines are too busy or too loud.

This genre thrives on simple melodic and harmonic features. Therefore, the chord changes in country music are generally quite simple, mostly consisting of I, IV, and V chords. For instance, if you are playing on a tune that's in the key of E, it will use the E chord (I), the A chord (IV), and the B7 chord (V). The V chord has a flatted seventh because its notes are derived from the "mother" key, in this case the notes of the key of E.

Some of the typical sounds the country fiddle might make come from old-time, bluegrass, and blues left- and right-hand techniques. Shuffle stroke, tasty slides, the percussive three-note lead-in, and the occasional flatting of the third and fifth tones, help create a stylistically appropriate quality. (See the pages 53, 59, and 82 for these techniques.)

To prepare for the tune, review your E, A, and B7 chord tones and scales:

Learn some of the double-stops that can be used from each of these chords to dress up your playing skills. Notice how I have selected and combined the primary chord tones (1 3 5) from each key to create a selection of double-stops. Practice these by tuning the lower note first, then the upper, and then cream them together.

There are a number of different kinds of slides used in country music that can just as easily be applied to blues, bluegrass, or jazz: 1) you can slide up into the pitch (variations in the width of the slide and the speed will change its effect); 2) you can slide up to pitch and then down out of it; or 3) you can hit the pitch on target and then spill down out of it:

Here's a line built on a sixth chord in the key of C. Notice how it starts with a flatted third, slides up to the natural third, and makes its way down to the sixth of the key. The second bar is like a mirror image, but leading <u>up</u> to the sixth. Try moving this line through some of the more popular "fiddle" keys: G, D, A, and E.

Moving in the interval of a sixth within your improvised line can be quite tasty in this style as well:

Listen to fiddlers like Buddy Spicher, Vassar Clements, and Mark O'Connor -- all of whom have made major contributions to what's referred to as the "Nashville sound" on fiddle -- to build your mastery of this fiddle style.

Ecclesiastes 9:10: Whatsoever thy hand findeth to do, do it with thy might!

Practice day and night. Scales in octaves, 3rd's, and 5th's especially in the keys of F#, C#, Ab, Bb and Eb. Always give the honor and glory to God and ask for help.

A good rhythm section is what you need. You're only as good as the weakest one who is backing you up. In turn help the weakest member of your band. Always try to make other people look and sound good. Learn the melody and the lyrics. Above all learn the chords. If you are backing someone up remember that playing less is good. If you play too much, you override the overall group and you're not being a team player. When backing someone up, compliment what they are saying.

Play from your heart and not from your mind. Most of all love your fellow musicians and give them the praise they need and encourage them in their musical attempts. Music is love.

- **Buddy Spicher**

After playing the melody, practice creating a "country" sound while soloing on the chord changes:

Country Ride
by Julie Lyonn Lieberman ©1999 Huiksi Music

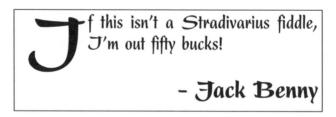

If this isn't a Stradivarius fiddle, I'm out fifty bucks!

- Jack Benny

Irish Reelies

Celtic fiddle tunes can be found at the root of many fiddle styles worldwide. The word *fidil* has been traced back in Ireland to an Irish poem *The Fair of Carnan*, from the eighth century. While we don't really know what the music of that time sounded like, we do have indications that the fidil and harp were used as an accompaniment to epic poems. Three hundred years later, a Welsh monk named Giraldus Cambrensis described the harp music as "…rapid and articulate yet at the same time sweet and pleasing."

When Crusaders brought back the three-stringed *rebec* from the East between 1096 and 1291, it's possible that the drone quality of the instrument influenced Irish music.

The family of viols were invented in the fifteenth century and became extremely popular until the invention of the violin in the seventeenth century. The family of viols (bass, tenor, and treble) are still used today to play Renaissance music, the literature they were intended for centuries ago.

Irish musicians were revered, and enjoyed high status in Irish culture until Elizabethan times, when musicians were imprisoned or executed for practicing their profession. This isn't surprising, when you consider just how deeply Irish music can reach its listeners. The musicians could have been considered dangerous, for the power of their music could inspire their audiences to take political action.

Today, there are thousands of Irish fiddle tunes that have been compiled and notated. If you get three professional fiddlers together, each may know upwards of hun-

dreds of tunes, but there may only be a handful that they know in common, depending upon which region of Ireland they grew up in, who they've learned from, and what circles they've traveled in!

Irish tunes work equally well at lightning tempos as they do at leisurely ones, so stay with what's comfortable for you, and slowly work your way up.

In addition to the slow form, the air, there are four forms used in Irish instrumental music:

double jig: 6/8 time:

single jig: 6/8 time:

slip jig: 9/8 time:

reel: 4/4 time:

While there are some delightful exceptions, almost every Irish tune is structured: AABB. This means that there are two sections, each made up of four measures. Each section repeats two times. Most of the tunes are in the keys of G, D, E (minor), and A (minor), with a few in C, F, and Bb.

When Irish musicians perform, they group tunes together into medleys. Sometimes an entire medley will be made up of tunes that are in the same key, and some medleys start with a slower tune and build up in speed, lay-ering in other instruments such as the bodhran (a frame drum hit with a stick), flute, guitar, or uileann pipes (a smaller version of the bagpipes).

There is little or no shifting into higher positions on the neck and little or no vibrato used for the faster tunes. The primary challenge for the left hand comes from the embellishments fiddlers add to the notes of the tune. These ornaments individualize each fiddler's interpretation. For instance, here is a phrase with six possible ways to "dress it up:"

Here are some popular Irish left-hand ornaments. Apply each ornament to the notes of a D minor scale.

D minor scale:

The right hand has to be able to quickly navigate constant string crossing and uses a **treble**, a fast bowed triplet that can tend to sound more like two sixteenth notes and an eighth:

Relax your fingers and wrist and try to originate the motion from your forearm as you apply a bowed treble to each note of the D minor scale. Use small bows.

Now practice changing pitch on the A string as you alternate playing the bowed treble on the open D string:

It is the variety of ornamentation and use of variation; the roll, the triplet, the rhythm of the bow, that makes Irish traditional fiddle music so unique. For those who seek the challenge of this journey, there is wonder and discovery around every musical corner..

- James Kelly

If you are a strong reader, then learn *Kia* by ear from the CD. If you are a weak reader, try to work it out visually first and then use the CD as a reinforcement.

After you play the melody a few times, try improvising with the notes of the D minor scale using some of the embellishments

that you have just learned.

Kia can be played at a wide range of tempos. While I generally perform this tune at a lively pace, we've provided you with a dreamy tempo to give you ample space to explore improvisation.

Kia
by Julie Lyonn Lieberman ©1997

GEANTRAIGHE - AN EXCITEMENT TO LOVE AND LAUGHTER

GOLTRAIGHE - AN AROUSAL TO VALOUR OR TEARS

SUANTRAIGHE - A DISPOSITION TO SLUMBER AND REPOSE

The music has been in constant motion between generations, between localities. It was transmitted aurally, and representation of the music was as faithful as one's memory and one's imagination would allow.

Musicians injected phrases and passages into tunes where they had forgotten pieces of melody. They made the tunes their own. People were being creative without use of the word creative. Composition is improvisation slowed down anyway.

In times before people needed to define their genre, they created as their heart felt. My affinity is with the soul of the music and the techniques involved are simply tools for that expression. The music is language for me. It's what you want to say that is of paramount importance.

- Martin Hayes

Drivin' To Cape Breton

In the early half of the 1800s, roughly 30,000 Scots were forced to leave the Highlands and Western Isles of Scotland. They traveled en masse to Cape Breton, which had sparse French settlements and Mi'kmaq Indians already living there. The Scots, of Celtic origin, far outnumbered their neighbors, and their language and fiddle tradition were preserved and flourished due to their many years of virtual isolation. Poor conditions on the roads in the early days even kept pockets of Scots communities isolated from each other.

Tunes were exchanged amongsingers, pipers, and fiddlers through *puirt a beul* (mouth music; also called *jiggling* in Irish). The rhythms and inflections of the Gaelic language informed the fiddler's touch and phrasing. While fiddling in Scotland went through Puritanical suppression by the religious leaders and later, displacement of the fiddle by the accordion, Breton fiddling remained intact and flourishes to this day.

Stepdancing, which became virtually extinct in Scotland, is also still active in Cape Breton, and foot stomping by the fiddler while playing provides an incredibly vigorous backdrop for the dancers. Piano accompaniment was added by the 1930s, but the tradition is primarily a solo one.

There are literally hundreds of great fiddlers from this tradition. Joe Cormier, Natalie MacMaster (who learned from her father, Buddy), and Ashley MacIsaac, have helped bring the style to international attention.

The tunes are based on major, mixolydian (called "modal"), and minor scales, and many tunes switch orientation mid-stream (major to modal or major to minor).

There are some wonderful bow techniques used in Cape Breton fiddling, like the use of double upbows either leaving the bow on the string or sometimes lifting it slightly off the string in between notes. In either case the notes sound separate.

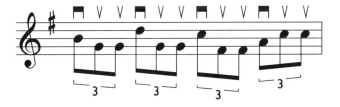

There is also a bowing called the whip-bow technique that whips the bow on the second of two notes during a slur. It's applied to a dotted rhythm.

The Cape Breton fiddlers use the Irish treble (triplet), but they call it a **cut**. They also use a grace note from the scale tone above down to the melody note, and call it a **pull-off**. The bowing arm is incredibly vigorous which most likely stems from the fact that the "band" used to accompany the dancers usually consists of one fiddler!

A typical approach to improvisation by a traditional Cape Breton player, might include the doubling or tripling of melody notes, adding bow techniques, or varying the placement of the left-hand embellishments.

The Cape Breton repertoire is made up of **marches**, **reels**, **jigs** and **strathspeys**. "Tullachgorum" -- one of my favorite tunes of this genre -- is a **strathspey**. This form is partially defined by its use of dotted rhythms, but we are going to start with the bare bones of the melody to help you familiarize yourself with the tune. We will layer style into it bit by bit to help ease the learning process!

IN LEAGUE WITH SCOTLAND, THE CAPE BRETON PASTOR FATHER KENNETH MACDONALD (1865 - 94), GATHERED UP ALL THE VIOLINS IN HIS PARISH AND DESTROYED THEM. HE AND OTHER CLERGY BELIEVED THAT FIDDLES AND PIPES WERE "INSTRUMENTS OF THE DEVIL." THE MUSIC FLOURISHED ANYWAY!

Tullachgorum
bare bones melody

Isolate the rhythm, applying it to a G7 scale. This scale is often called "modal" because the seventh degree of the scale is flatted.

Once you've mastered the rhythmic phrase, apply it to the melody.

Tullachgorum
melody with dotted rhythms

The symbol you see below is a Cape Breton ornament. It is called a **warble**. ⋇ The working finger plays the note, partially releases the string from the fingerboard, and then restores the finger pressure. Listen to recordings to capture its timing.

Isolate the finger motion on each of the notes of a G7 scale, and then try to apply it to some of the notes of the melody that have a relatively longer value.

For improvisation in this style, use the notes of the G7 modal scale, as well as the open G and D as drone strings. Incorporate the strathspey's rhythmic phrasing, as well as some of the left- and

right-hand techniques we've discussed as you invent new melodies against the accompaniment.

For the most complete version of the tune we'll add in the double-stops. Keep your bow pressure light and practice each mea- sure slowly for intonation. You can then go back and add in some warbles and some of the bow strokes we've discussed.

Tullachgorum
traditional tune -- full melody

Track Nine

A lot of fiddlers I run into play different styles. My experience has always been very different. There were no other styles where I was growing up. I have only been exposed to Cape Breton fiddling. Playing in the Cape Breton style is a natural part of me from growing up surrounded by the music and all the elements of the culture.

I've obviously been traveling a lot and I have all sorts of music interests and have been intro- duced to violinists I would never have heard otherwise. As a result of hearing different violin- ists, like Mark O'Connor and Darol Anger, as well as pop and Celtic music, I have a desire to be able to adapt what I do. I don't want to change what I play. I don't want to learn other styles. What sets me apart is what I do now, but there are things I've done to the Cape Breton style to make it more the Natalie MacMaster style. Every fiddler has done that. You can't help but make the music your own.

What's beautiful about the style is its natural drive and flow. It's a music that is rough around the edges, not overly polished. The strength of the music lies in the feel of it and the rhythm. The rhythm comes from the dancing. To play Cape Breton, you should focus on the bowing. You've got to put the rhythm into the bow and use slurs only where necessary.

- Natalie MacMaster

Fiddle It French

Today, we have the Acadian fiddle music of the Maritime Provinces (Nova Scotia), the Québecois fiddling of French Canada, the Franco-American fiddle music of New England, and the Cajun/Zydeco fiddle styles of Louisiana. The music originally came from Celtic roots, but took some major twists and turns along the way via the French!

In the early 1600s, hundreds of French settlers arrived in the Maritime provinces of Canada (Nova Scotia, New Brunswick, and Prince Edward Island), calling their colony Acadia, or *Acadie* in French. Historians believe that between 1654 and 1755 the Acadian population grew from 300-350 colonists to about 12,000-15,000. The French dominated the cultural landscape even with a healthy level of intermarriage between them and the English, Scottish, Irish, Spanish, Basque, and Mi'kmaq Indians.

In 1755 the British expelled the Acadians by force in what came to be known as Le Grand Dérangement (The Great Disturbance). Contrary to popular belief, the British deported only about 6,050 Acadians by ship, the remainder seeking refuge in nearby territories. Regardless, some sources claim that about half the pre-expulsion Acadian population died during the expulsion.

About 2,600 to 3,000 Acadians sailed to Louisiana between 1765 and 1785 to begin their lives anew. On this inhospitable land, some of the Acadian exiles and their descendants intermarried with other ethnic groups (mainly French, Portuguese, Spanish, German, African, and Anglo-American settlers), developing new identities over time.

Meanwhile, other Acadian exiles found refuge in present-day Canada and abroad; those in Canada still describe themselves as Acadians. The word is used less commonly in Louisiana because of the popularity of the term and identity "Cajun," which generally is not considered synonymous with Acadian.

In addition, an estimate in the 1980s identified some 20,000 persons of Acadian ancestry in the New England states, particularly Maine, which directly borders Canada's Maritime Provinces. It is estimated that today there are between 700,000 and 1.5 million Acadians worldwide (including Cajuns).

While the names of the tunes vary between French, Scottish, and Irish (you can easily hear "Scotch Waltz," "Pigeon on the Gate," and "Reel du Cordonnier" in the same evening), the Acadian fiddlers of the Maritime Provinces perform Irish and Scottish **reels** and **jigs**; **set-tunes** (cut-time tunes for set or square dancing but thought of in a separate category from reels); **waltzes** (3/4 time); **hornpipes** (medium tempo tunes that lilt the eighth notes); **marches** (played at a walking tempo); **airs** (rubato instrumental ballads); and **strathspeys** (4/4 medium tempo tunes that use dotted rhythms).

Cajun Fiddling

The Acadians brought the fiddle to Louisiana during their migration between 1765 and 1785. The diatonic accordion (from Germany), guitar (from Spain), and drums didn't become a part of the music until the 1900s. The fiddle usually maintains the basic tuning system (G, D, A, E) but when playing with a C accordion adapts to a cross-tuning (F, C, G, D).

Please keep in mind that none of these tunes were notated until the mid-1900s, so we're dealing with an oral tradition that produced all kinds of variations on the original repertoire, including mixing parts from two different tunes, new names, or new tunes that echoed qualities from vaguely remembered tunes.

Since the Cajuns were highly isolated for many years, the music had a chance to develop organically out of the culture; it was a culture built on teamwork for survival. Regular social gatherings and community dances at the end of a long, hard workweek gave everyone an opportunity to celebrate life, coming together to forget their troubles. Before the addition of the other instruments, it was the fiddler who, between his highly rhythmic use of the bow and stomping foot, invigorated the souls of the community enough to inspire them to dance and keep on a'dancin'!

Shuffle stroke, double-stops using an open string as a drone, bluesy slides, and playing a low melody or chords with a driving rhythmic back-beat against the regular melody line (on a second fiddle, which is called "bassing" or "seconding") all help distinguish the Cajun fiddle sound. Please refer to the Irish, old-time, and blues units, to develop these left- and right-hand techniques.

There are several rhythmic/melodic motifs that can be found throughout Cajun music which can be used during improvisation in this style. The use of a triplet figure that

loops back through itself, giving a "hurry up and wait" sensibility (almost like a tumble) to the eighth note figures, and the tendency to repeat pitches within a shuffle stroke phrase all help define the style:

Zydeco Fiddling

Described as a mixture of French, blues, jazz, and rhythm and blues, Zydeco music was created and is performed by Creole musicians. The term Creole is used to describe descendants of French, Spanish, Portuguese,

Well, it helps to be from Louisiana. Cajun is a bluesy laid back style that's got drone imaging from medieval France, Creole rhythm, and a swing mentality.

- Michael Doucet

and African ancestry. Slaves were brought to Louisiana from West Africa sometime between 1719 and 1809. Haitian immigrants all settled in Louisiana, and French planters exiled from Cuba brought Caribbean French slaves with them in 1810.

The Cajuns had little interest in slavery and worked side by side with blacks as tenant farmers. The French and African languages blended together to form a new language, also called Creole. Early Creole music con-sisted of ballad singing, hand clapping, and rhythmic foot stomping. The black Creoles were among the first to learn the accordion when it made its appearance in Louisiana. While the fiddle style was mostly informed by white Cajun traditions, the bluesy element of slide technique can be attributed to black culture. The first Creole to record was black fiddler Douglas Bellard, and Canray Fontenot is the Zydeco fiddler of greatest renown.

Dance Doucet Dance
by Julie Lyonn Lieberman ©1999 Huiksi Music

French-Canadian music is a Celtic music, like Irish, like Cape Breton, like Scottish or French Breton (medieval-sounding from Brittany). They are all from the same root, and should be considered Celtic. You must not lose sight of that.

The French-Canadian and the Irish lived next door to each other in Canada. The German accordion mixing with the French-Canadian syncopation, mixing with the Irish ornamentation...

French fiddling almost has a Latin feel to it (because of the underlying syncopation). You're accentuating the off-beat, and you're taking some of those off-beats and you're making them even more accented.

Québecois and Franco-American fiddling are quite similar. The fiddle's job is to dance the tune and tell the dancer's feet what to do. The use of the bow, the style itself, is a little more percussive than Irish music and the bow is a little more off the string than the Irish use.

A lot of ornaments start on a bouncing upbow, a very staccato upbow. While someone coming to it from a classical background would find the bowing easy to pick up, they would have difficulty with the upbeat accents of the rhythm. The accents have to go where the feet need to go for the dancers. You have to hear the dancing feet as you play.

Playing the dance phrases so that they fit into the dance that's being danced, you have to keep your ears and eyes open. You're listening to the rhythm of their feet on the floor to know how to phrase it.

Acadian tunes tend to roll more; the edges are harder. The Franco-American tunes and the Québecois tunes both jump. That's what the difference is. And French-Canadian waltzes are the Viennese of this continent. Texas waltzes are wonderful but they don't dance the way the French waltzes dance.

I started in 1972 with one band, and rejuvenated New England dancing in Boston. We've gone from 10 registered groups running dances in New England in 1972 to 400 nationwide. I'm French and I live in New England, and both are reflected in the music I play.

It's all dancing for me: finding the rhythms and dancing on the tune so that the dancers can find them too. It's just so much fun to get it right. It doesn't matter what style it is. It's just so much fun!

- Donna Hébert

Franco-American and Québecois Style

As we've seen from all of the fiddle styles discussed in this book, the tunes in all fiddle cultures developed as partner to dance. According to fiddler Donna Hébert, there are bodies of Franco-American tunes that are used with specific types of dances. These dance forms include *lancers*, *quadrilles*, *cotillions*, *longways* (line-facing-line dances); *square form* (same as a quadrille); and *circle* (circle dance).

Many of the tunes are in 2/4, with some in 6/8 (mainly single jigs) and some in 4/4 in the older traditions (quadrilles and lancers). Most of the tunes follow a 32-bar form but then there are what Donna refers to as the unsquare, crooked tunes. "I play French tunes that fit the 32-bar phrase for dances, but I'd say that 30% to 40% of the French tunes are crooked. God bless them. Not a straight 4 x 8; they'll add an extra beat or put three beats in one measure!"

There are two primary ways of punching up the notes in the phrase. Try applying each to a G major scale for practice:

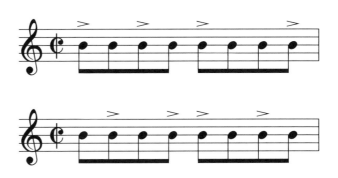

Fireside
traditional tune as notated by Donna Hébert

Dancin' Scandi

My first experience playing fiddle tunes from Scandinavia was back in the early 80s, when Jay Ungar hired a dream band of fiddlers (yours truly, Matt Glaser, Evan Stover, and Kenny Kosek, to name a few) to play at Liv Ullman's birthday party held at Bloomingdales in White Plains, NY. To this day, I don't think anyone at that party realized who the cute fiddlers were, wearing red vests and aprons courtesy of Bloomingdales!

Even though we use the term "Scandinavian Fiddling" to sum up the fiddle styles of Sweden, Norway, Denmark, and Finland, there are actually a number of differences between the regional styles of each of the these countries. Let's look at some of the similarities.

The melodies of Scandinavian fiddle tunes are built on major, minor and harmonic minor scales:

The use of a drone by bowing on two strings; open tunings (by retuning the violin strings to A - E - A - E or A - E - A - C♯) that use an open string as a drone against the melody; rhythmic bowing; left-hand ornamentation such as the use of grace notes or trills; and the subtle bending of pitch close to a quarter tone below concert pitch (akin to the use of blue notes in the blues); are all qualities that you can find in the music of Scandinavia.

The older bowed instruments, such as the Swedish **nyckelharpa** (keyed fiddle), the **strakharpa** (bowed harp), and the Norwegian **Hardingfele** (**Hardanger fiddle**), are still in use. The European violin didn't become popular in Scandinavia until the mid-17th century when French violinists were employed at the Swedish royal court.

As is the case with most fiddle music, Scandinavian fiddlers accompany dancers, and even stand in the middle of the dance floor, instead of apart from the dancers. Fiddler have to build rhythm into the melody through the use of the bow and the exuberant tapping of their feet in order to provide the dancers with an invigorating accompaniment. The rhythmic dance of the bow helps distinguish Scandi fiddling.

It's interesting to see how larger dance halls (rather than small kitchens or people's backyards) as well as recordings and radio have altered certain aspects of the music. For instance, in small spaces, the dancers could take smaller steps, and the tempos could go as fast as 130 up to 145. In larger dance halls, the tempo had to come down to accommodate larger dance steps.

The separation of the music from dance through recordings has encouraged the addition of fancier ornamentation such as long trills, as well as harmony played by several fiddles. Some fiddlers play the melody while others create a dancy rhythmic push behind the melody, using harmony notes, usually a third below the melody, or droning on the tonic and/or chord tones of the key.

There are a number of different styles found in Scandinavian fiddle literature, such as *mazurka*, *waltz*, *hambo*, and *schottische*. But the *polska* can be found throughout. The first time I saw the term "polska," I thought it was a typo. I just assumed that they were referring to the "polka," a fast dance performed in 2/4 time, which was introduced to Sweden in the 1860s. The polska is in 3/4 and the music works with the three beats in a distinctive manner.

Waltzes in American fiddle literature place emphasis on the first beat of the measure: **one** two three, whereas in the polska, you must think **three---&one** two!

Let's prepare for the Langbacka-Jans polska by first practicing its rhythmic pattern. The polska uses a dotted eighth note followed by a sixteenth. While classical musicians would tend to play that figure literally, Scandi fiddlers hold the dotted eighth longer. Leif Alpsjö gives two examples of how this might be written, but stresses that you must listen to the style to truly capture the rhythmic phrasing.

Try applying this rhythm to a D major scale:

Leif has kindly supplied us with a series of Scandi ornaments that can be applied to melody notes. Practice applying each type of ornament to each note of the D major scale:

The main purpose of our folk music is to move your feet to it, dancing or walking. When newcomers to Swedish folk music play a polska, they think simple and straight; they think that 3/4 is 3/4. It is not 3/4! It holds endless subtle possibilities. It is very artistic and when well performed it is wonderful to dance to, often very sensual.

Naturally the subtle rhythms of the old music were compromised down to more basic rhythms in the group music. When the accordion entered the Swedish dance floors around 1860, it also obliterated a lot of the old subtlety both the way it was played and with the more straight mazurka-like polska repertoire.

The tempo in the back of your mind may be a very even 1 - 2 - 3, but on top of that the rhythm is quite varied and not played the simple way it is written. You may think of the 3/4 beat as oval - as an egg. The hambo (like the waltz) is less oval, almost round, while polskas are more oval depending on the local dialect and the dancing style.

If you only have the written music without a recording to listen to, think of the beat as 3 - 1 where the "and" of the third beat is very, very short. The first note of the third beat must be played long enough to drive the dancers efficiently around. This note is mostly played too short by inexperienced fiddlers and then the music turns into hambo or mazurka. The sixteenth note just before you play on beat 1 is so short, that it will appear more like a grace note to beat 1. That's why I say: think 3 - 1 instead of hambo-like 1 - 3. That's when polska playing is turning into an art.

Waltz, hambo and mazurka are in 3/4 and schottisch and polka in 2/4 or 4/4. They are completely different styles and cannot be compared.

As I see it, the bowing should be easygoing, elegant, and precise, expressing your temperament, taste, and the best rhythm that you can give to the audience and the dancers.

Leif means "the inheritor." I like that very much as I see myself as a tradition-bearer. Somebody recently said that playing the nyckelharpa is like playing a cathedral. I agree, especially if you have a good instrument.

- Leif Alpsjö

Langbacka-Jans Polska

traditional tune as notated by Leif Alpsö

Bluesy Blues

Some scratchy 78 recordings and old newspaper ads are almost all that remains of the legacy of African-American slave musicians who learned that excellence on an instrument like the fiddle might provide them with a slightly gentler life than that of a field hand. While slaves were trained to play Western European classical and folk music publicly, they used the violin to express the music that was developing out of the Afro-American experience -- the blues -- during their private time. It isn't surprising that the violin and voice were the earliest instruments involved in playing the blues. The violin easily adapted itself to this art form because of its ability to match the human voice: both can slide in and out of pitch, smearing and bending notes with intense emotion.

For many decades following emancipation, hundreds of black fiddlers maintained the art of fiddling the blues throughout the South. Their use of syncopation and slide technique even had an influence on some of the old-time repertoire played by white Southern fiddlers. By the early 30s, there were over 50 recorded blues fiddlers. Players fortunate enough to be recorded, like Lonnie Johnson, Lonnie Chatmon, and Henry "Son" Sims, left us the gift of their creativity via improvisation on what had, up until that time, been an extremely traditional instrument.

These fiddlers were the forefathers of jazz violin. Without these old recordings, we would barely know the tradition had even existed, because it disappeared quite suddenly, leaving less than a handful of players, namely Howard Armstrong and Butch Cage, to carry the tradition on through the century.

Most of the recorded blues fiddlers migrated to cities where many of them found work playing for silent films because the violin couldn't be heard in noisy bars. They earned high enough wages from their work to buy houses and live well. When the talking films came out, they were all put out of work.

Bassist Milt Hinton, while delivering newspapers as a boy in the suburbs of Chicago, made quite a discovery: "...*And on their screened-in back porches, they [blues fiddlers] were rolling cigars...making cigars, and taking them downtown to sell them to the wealthy people in the downtown department stores. This is how they survived when they didn't have work. This is what they had to do to hold on to their homes.*"

There are certain generalizations we can make about the techniques these violinists evolved to move the instrument into a new stylistic framework. Classical techniques like vibrato and tremolo were modified to play the blues: the width and speed of the vibrato became more varied and less symmetrically measured, and tremolo became a fast, tight blues shimmer. Various slide techniques were developed, and, of course, each player used improvisation as the basis of the style.

Some adaptations are more difficult to verbalize in detail due to their extreme subtlety. For instance, rather than attacking notes in a symmetrical, crisp fashion, the use of the bowing arm, coupled with a left-hand slide technique, created an effect that was more like a snake ambling and slithering its way along. Rhythmic emphasis shifted from the symmetrical, straight rhythms of classical music to swung and syncopated phrasing.

Today, most jazz violinists know how to play the blues, but few specialize in this richly expressive style. The era of the blues fiddler is long gone. Keep the art alive by incorporating this style into your repertoire.

Learning to play the blues provides an excellent vehicle for classical players who want to break away from the music stand and transition into a whole new way of thinking and hearing. Even one's sense of touch on the instrument can change. This art form is a vital, deeply expressive genre, and learning to play the blues creates a supportive stylistic, harmonic, and technical foundation for playing swing, jazz, pop, and rock music.

To begin to assimilate this style, there are three changes you will have to make: 1) To get started, forget that you ever knew how to use vibrato! There's nothing worse than a classical player trying to play the blues while vibrating sweetly on every note. Later, you can learn how to control and vary the width and speed of your vibrato, using it as a seasoning instead of as the "main course;" 2) lighten your left-hand touch on the fingerboard to prepare your-self for incorporating slide technique into your playing; and, 3) imprint the 12-bar (12- measure) blues form into your psyche by listening to recordings. If you're a total beginner at improvisation, you can get started by using the scale tones from the key that the blues is in. Look at the key signature or the first chord symbol to determine the key, and then use a diatonic (seven-note) scale in that key, but flat the seventh note of the scale. The "7" in the chord symbol indicates a dominant seventh chord, which is "jazz hieroglyphics" for lowering the seventh of the key.

For the purpose of learning, we will be focussing on the blues form in the key of Bb. This is a popular key for jazz musicians, because Bb is to horn players what C is to the pianist. Once you are comfortable improvising in this key, you can apply the following exercises to any of the twelve keys because the form and guidelines will remain the same. (E blues is popular in folk music.)

The gentlest approach to improvising on the blues is to start with a country blues. All blues use a 12-bar structure, and vary the

The Blues is the common thread that runs through all popular music: jazz, rock, even country and folk. That's what attracts everyone whether they realize it or not. It's more than a scale, or a chord progression, or a groove. It's a feeling that touches every person on the planet. I can play Ellington, the Allman Brothers, Gershwin, The Grateful Dead, and a fiddle tune in any show and have it all fit together because blues lives in all of it."

- Randy Sabien

complexity of the chords. The country blues is the simplest form. What you see below is a chord progression that an improvising player might use as a basis for their improvisation without even needing to see a melody line written in:

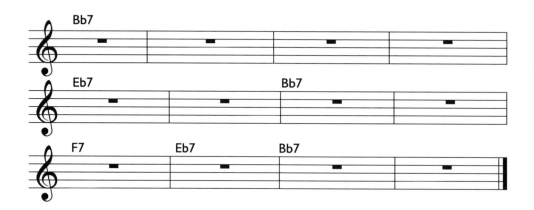

As a first step towards improvisation in this form, you can use any of the following variations of the Bb scale and ignore the chord changes. The first scale is based on a Bb7 chord, lowering the seventh of the scale. The second scale provides you with the option of flatting the third or the fifth, in addition to the regular scale tones. The third scale is called a "pentatonic scale," because it is a five-note scale that omits the second and sixth tones.

In blues and jazz, the key signature only applies to the melody. Once you start to improvise -- if you wish to create a more sophisticated improvisation than outlined above -- you must follow the chord symbols.

Each chord symbol will tell you what key to play in, what type of scale to use, and for how long. So, to create a more advanced improvisation, you will need to learn the primary chord tones (1 3 5 b7) and scales of the other chords in the piece. Think of each chord change like a coded road map; each will guide your ears and left hand into in a new tonal center. In jazz, the chord tones are important to emphasize while improvising; they are the pillars of the improvisation. The other notes of the scale are vehicles to carry you to and away from the chord tones in new and interesting ways. Here are the chord and scale tones for the other two tonal centers in the Bb country blues:

Since you will need to be able to access this family of keys on split second notice anywhere on your instrument in any order, it is to your advantage to practice scrambling the notes. For instance:

3 1 5 3 1 b7 5 3 1

3 2 1 5 4 3 b7 6 5

You can also practice moving short melodic riffs through the chord changes:

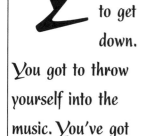

You got to get down. You got to throw yourself into the music. You've got to make that violin scratch and moan.
— **Papa John Creach**

Perhaps you are beginning to notice that an improvising violinist has to know all twelve keys equally, as well as all the chord forms and their accompanying scales. You also have to be able to remember the chord sequence in any given piece of music while inventing original music instantaneously. Whoever said that improvising musicians were inferior to classical musicians?

"Papa Blues" is based on a slightly more complex blues structure. Notice that there are many more chords (called "chord changes" or "changes" in jazz terminology) to keep track of. Here are the additional scales:

Fm7

Dm7b5

G7

Cm7

F7

Dm7

When you are dealing with a structure like the blues, it's far better to learn the chord changes based on structure rather than reading the actual key symbols. Start working on this tune by thinking through the chords based on a numbering system in relationship to the key of Bb. The slashes indicate the number of beats.

This is harder work initially, but will enable you to translate this same structure into any of the twelve keys so that if you're at a jam session you won't be restricted to any one key.

I////	IV////	I////	Vm7//I//
IV7////	////	I7////	IIIm7b5//VI//
IIm7///	V7///	III//VI//	IIm7//V7//

Papa Blues
by Julie Lyonn Lieberman ©1999 Huiksi Music

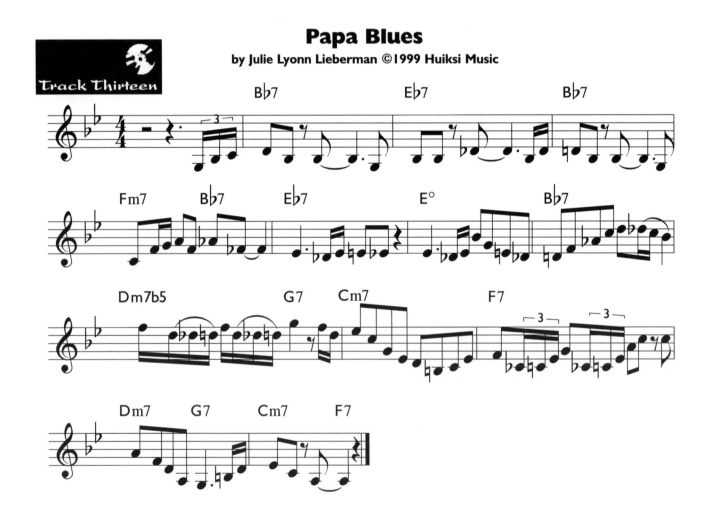

Swinging Fancy

Whether it's the swinging double fiddles of the Bob Wills band from the late 30s and early 40s, or the swinging "tear it up" early jazz violinists such as Joe Venuti, Eddie South, Stuff Smith, and Stephane Grappelli, to today's Claude "Fiddler" Williams, the violin has been integral to swing music for close to a century.

The two most distinctive elements of this upbeat music are actually found in its rhythmic components. The emphasis within the four-beat measure is on the second and fourth beat, and improvisation, though it can include any type of rhythmic figure, is predominantly comprised of swinging eighth notes.

Swing violin is probably one of the hardest styles for classical players to adapt to! Many classical violinists try to swing by playing dotted eighth notes. You can best create the swing rhythm by tying two eighth-note triplets and playing the third triplet separately, but in general, using the swing bowings and listening to a lot of recordings is the best route into the swing sound because if you approach the rhythm with too much analysis you might tend to sound mechanical or stiff.

Swing music is built on a 32-bar form. The structure is divided as follows: A A B A Each section is made up of eight measures. Most of the earlier swing players used a sweet, classical vibrato when playing swing, but it isn't a necessary ingredient.

Here are some preparatory exercises you can use to begin to develop this style:

1) When you practice swinging your eighth notes, use small bows.

2) To get the feel of the swing pulse, try counting 1 2 3 4 with an emphasis on the one while clapping only on the second and fourth beats.

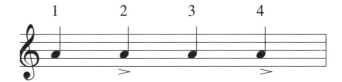

J do my best to make my violin sound like a horn. J came up around horn players like Charlie Parker, Lester Young, Ben Webster (what a hell of a tenor player), and J always liked Louis Armstrong. J think of the changes a horn would play, the different chords a horn would play, and J make my violin sound like that.

- Claude Williams

3) Apply the following bowing patterns to a two- or three-octave scale. Then try improvising in that key using run-on eighth notes. Notice how these bowings emphasize inflection (natural accentuation through a change in bow direction) on the weak part of the beat.

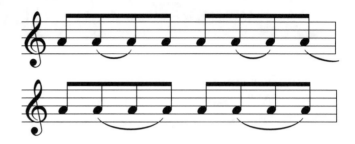

The following swing progression is a fairly typical one. Like the blues, we're learning a structure that can be applied to any key. When musicians say, "let's play rhythm changes," this is the progression they are referring to. You can find this progression in all 12 keys on Jazz Aids, Volume 47 (see **References**).

When you are ready to improvise on this structure, start by creating an improvisation using half notes to give yourself a chance to create a well-architected line. Then move on to quarter-note, eighth-note, triplet, sixteenth-note, and mixed rhythm improvisations.

wing fiddle means that one is playing violin in the tradition of Louis Armstrong, with his profound new ideas about the human experience of time, and his ability to joyfully communicate life energy. Playing swing on the violin should make people happy.

To me the most wildly swinging fiddle player of all time is Stuff Smith. Ultimately swing fiddle is about rhythm and the groove, with an overlay of hip ideas added on top.

- Matt Glaser

The tune that follows has been built on the chord changes of an old jazz standard, rather than the rhythm changes outlined on the previous page. After learning the melody, review the chord tones and chordal scales of each chord change before soloing.

Track Fourteen

Georgia Swing

by Julie Lyonn Lieberman ©1999 Huiksi Music

BeBoppin'

By the mid 40s, a new music could be heard in jazz clubs and recording studios. It had faster tempos, different harmonies, and new rhythms. You couldn't dance to it. Nor could you sing along. Perhaps this accounts for why bop never became as popular a music as swing.

Historians describe the birth of bebop as occurring in a Harlem nightclub called Minton's Playhouse where trumpeter Dizzy Gillespie, pianist Thelonius Monk, drummer Kenny Clarke, guitarist Charlie Christian, and later, saxophonist Charlie Parker (who became the chief proponent of bebop) invented this genre during a series of jam sessions in the early forties.

Clearly, after over a decade of swing music, the public (as well as jazz musicians) were overly saturated and it was time for something new. Latin music was beginning to infiltrate the jazz scene, introducing new rhythmic concepts, and there were already hints in the evolution of jazz of what was to come.

> I think it's becoming increasingly recognized that Stuff Smith was a great jazz musician and the equal of his peers: Coleman Hawkins, Lester Young, Art Tatum, Ben Webster, Red Allen, Roy Eldridge -- you name them-- he's the same as them.
>
> The other point that hasn't been recognized, although I think it's becoming increasingly more recognized now, is that he is an important figure in the development of bebop. Dizzy Gillespie was a very close friend of his, as a youngster. Of course there were others: Dom Bias, Lucky Thompson, and Coleman Hawkins, who used a lot of the bebop musicians in their younger days. Stuff was one of those who certainly Dizzy turned to very much for inspiration and advice, and Dizzy himself acknowledged that.
>
> - **Anthony Barnett**

Stuff Smith's wildly unpredictable and energetic playing style had foreshadowed and reflected this development in jazz. But he was the exception. When bebop struck, violinists didn't know what had happened. They were not prepared for the complex rhythms and harmonies of bebop. Like Grappelli, most of the early players stuck with blues and swing styles. Charlie Parker had generated a revolution in jazz. But, with the exception of Stuff Smith and Joe Kennedy, Jr., few fiddlers attempted to incorporate bop into their repertoire. With the earlier players staying firmly implanted in the harmonic, rhythmic, and melodic concepts of swing, they were conspicuously absent from bebop. For this reason, the violin was less visible in jazz during the 40s and early 50s.

Aside from Smith and Kennedy, it would take several decades for even a few violinists to brave the complexities of bop. Elek Bascik made two albums in honor of Charlie Parker in the 70s, but there was little improvisation. And Jean-Luc Ponty's first album, *Sunday Walk* (1972), was a classic. But, despite critical acclaim for this bebop, recording, Ponty chose to play jazz fusion.

Today, there are few violinists that successfully focus on this genre, choosing rather to borrow elements from it, and incorporate those elements into their playing style.

Bop uses eighths, triplets, and sixteenth note runs. This style is distinguished by the use of chromatic passing tones. Notice how the addition of a chromatic passing tone alters how and when the player lands on a primary chord tone in relationship to the beat:

Lines can change direction abruptly, sometimes making large interval leaps…

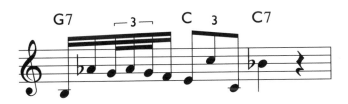

Many classic bop melodies, called "lines," have been written over the chord changes of popular jazz standards. Often, the chords were embellished upon. Flatting the five of the chord became popular, much as the lowering of the third and seventh in blues and swing had emerged in earlier years.

Another innovation in bebop soloing, was the idea of delaying one's entrance. Instead of coming in at the top of the chorus (the first beat of the 32-bar form), the soloist might wait and start their improvised phrase in the middle of an eight-bar section, and finish that phrase past the traditional point of completion. This method echoes the African approach to circular structures, where each layer of percussion treats the first beat -- the "downbeat" -- of the measure as inferred, and creates musical phrases that start and end staggered into that framework.

The predictability of the swing rhythm, with its emphasis on the two and the four, was replaced by accents in surprising patterns. For instance:

Swing

Bop

Try practicing inflections (accents) on a G major scale. To create a smooth inflection that's embedded into the phrase, do not tense your arm muscle or jerk your hand. Keep "ice-skating" the bow in a horizontal motion, and gently lean in towards your index finger each time you wish to add an inflection. It's best to understate your accents, because many players overwork them at first. If you feel strained in any way, take that as a clue that you are working way too hard!

For a more challenging workout, repeat all of the rhythmic accentuations notated below, but subdivide each beat into four mentally, and enter on the second 16th, the third, and then the fourth 16th.

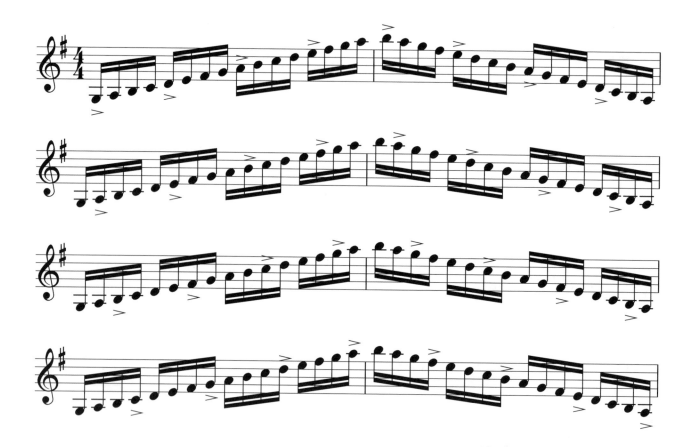

In playing bebop at the end of World War II, it was a marvelous thing to learn the musical characteristics of Dizzy Gillespie, Charlie Parker, and Thelonius Monk, like the flatted fifth, the flatted ninth, and clusters (foreign tones or notes outside of the scale).

I think that I have been more influenced by horns than the keyboard. I'm hearing horns. I'm trying to emulate horns. We improve our listening skills when we try to emulate style by transferring a horn line to the violin. My contention is that a lot of players don't realize -- as far as jazz violin is concerned -- the matter of breathing. When I shape my phrases, I'm listening in terms of breathing.

- Joe Kennedy, Jr.

The following tune has been built on the same chord changes as the first half of *Georgia Swing* (page 89) to give you a chance to compare the tremendous difference that can be created within each style on the same chord changes.

Bop Bird Bop
by Julie Lyonn Lieberman ©1999 Huiksi Music

Lively Latin

Violinists are relative babies in the field of Latin music. It is an open playing field, an undiscovered country! There is so much potential here for amazing rhythmic phrases, interesting repetitive patterns across the strings, and double-stop work. This genre is just waiting for adventurous players to explore it.

Traditionally speaking, the violin in Latin music is most typically used in charanga bands(not to be confused with the Mexican mariachi band, which also uses the violin). This style of music was created in Cuba and arrived in New York in the 50s. It is dance music that features a vocalist accompanied by a percussion set (using two tuneable drums, cowbells, cymbal, and woodblocks called *timbales*), the Cuban conga drum, a contrabass, a gourd called a *guiro* (which is scraped with a stick), flute, piano, and violin(s). The vocals normally are interspersed with hot flute improvisations -- all against a background of repeated violin figures usually played by two to four violins. A

typical violin figure might go something like this:

The violins' parts are heavily arranged, using rests in surprising spots (at least surprising to the novice) and sudden changes in their lines, sometimes moving from repetitive rhythmic figures to lush long tones. There is some soloing, but they are mostly relegated to a subservient role to the vocalist and flutist.

We are not going to focus on charanga, though, because I'm more interested in offering you some suggestions and patterns designed to help you explore and develop a new role for the violin in Latin music.

The term "Latin Music" is deceptive because it infers that it includes all Spanish-speaking countries. It doesn't. Each country in South America, its surrounding islands, and each of the other Spanish-speaking countries, such as Spain, and Mexico, has developed its own distinctive music, shaped by local history and diverse populations such as indigenous cultures, Africans imported through slavery, and immigrants from Europe.

When we use the term "Latin Music," we are really referring to Afro-Cuban and Brazilian music because of their influence on jazz and

---

Learn to dance the steps that the music accompanies. That really helped me to play in a salsa band. In salsa bands that use strings (charanga orquestas), the violinist must develop a storehouse of short (one- or two-measure) montuno patterns. For these you need to understand how to fit a riff into the clave rhythm.

The violin is primarily a rhythm instrument in salsa, so prepare to enjoy being a cog in a big rhythm machine. Eighths are not swung and there is not much slurring. There is so much rhythm going on that solos are generally sparse, but rhythmically hip.

- **Stacy Phillips**

their presence in the pop mainstream.

Afro-Cuban music is shaped around a clave rhythm. Each instrument in the band, whether it's keyboard, percussion or bass, keeps its own rhythmic phrase going, and all of these phrases layer on top of each other, but the focal phrase is the clave.

Forward clave: 3 & 2

Reverse clave: 2 & 3

African clave

What does this mean to the string player? The rhythms layered in by the various percussion instruments used (timbales, congas, bongos, guiro, cowbell), as well as the rhythm section (guitar, piano, bass), are highly syncopated, and may not bring out the down beat -- particularly the "one " of each measure. Many string players get lost and confused as to where they are within the measure or how to shape the rhythmic phrases of their improvisation.

Since most string players tend to train so that their bow arm is actually a servant to the pitch line created by the left hand, the development of the bow hand as an independent operator is often neglected. Yet in Latin music, rhythmic mastery over the bow hand is essential.

Research has revealed that the rhythmic center of the brain is actually located in a separate location from the pitch center. Isolating the bow arm for fifteen to thirty minutes a day will enable you to access and develop the rhythmic center, creating a tremendously masterful bow arm in general, and a keen command over rhythmic response in particular.

A drummer can hit the drum with their hand and let the sound ring out by quickly lifting off the drum. But if he or she leaves their hands on the drum after the hit, a different quality of sound ensues. String players can create a staccato sound a number of ways. We can bounce the bow, we can create a bite (martélé) on the front of an elongated note, or we can use short, evenly accentuated, clipped bows. In this case, a notated eighth note will sound more like a sixteenth note followed by a rest, and there is a lighter quality to how the bow moves on the string then with martélé.

Using an open string, practice mastering this "clipped" sound. It can be extremely effective in Latin music. As you develop your skill using this bow-stroke, you will be able to sustain it even at fast tempos. It's valuable to practice it in the typical fashion, alternating direction, as well as while moving in a continuous direction. This approach to phrasing, once successfully mastered, can then be combined with long tones.

String Crossing: Paradiddles

Percussionists create many incredible rhythmic effects by alternating sticks or hands on the same or combinations of percussion instruments. By assigning varying numbers of repetitions to each hand, they create tonal differences that enhance their rhythmic latticework. I've seen very little use of this by instrumentalists. Even though we don't have a collection of instruments at our disposal the way a percussionist does, there are ways to access the use of the sound quality of the paradiddle. Violinists tend to hear in linear, melodic phrases. To counterbalance this, it's helpful to develop a command over lines that require string alternation. Here are a few exercises to assist you.

Let's work with a clave rhythm to experiment with new possibilities for the use of the bow. Start by playing a clipped eighth note on your open D string, and tap on the body of the violin with your left hand to mark the rests.

Continue to use the D string to mark the notated eighth, and use the open A string to mark the rests.

In the next three examples, you'll see how I have incrementally added rhythms onto the notated D. I've replaced some eighths with two sixteenths, or with sixteenth-note triplets. This is challenging to the bow arm, because it sets up asymmetrical rhythmic patterns. Stay relaxed, start slowly, and repeat these phrases as long as it takes for you to bow them automatically. Your motor cortex is learning new movement sequences, and it may take a little while before your ears are able to recognize the pattern like an old friend.

As we discussed earlier, strings players are trained to lead with the left hand and to hear and create melodic lines. To create an atypical, rhythmically interesting sound on the violin while soloing, you must develop as much rhythmic facility in the bow arm as possible. The more phrases you isolate and practice, the better.

Pedal Point

A pedal point is a repeated pitch (or, in this case, double-stop) that alternates with a moving line. It can create an enjoyable effect by providing the ear with a reference point against which melodic and rhythmic motion can take place:

Octaves

In Latin music, it is typical for the pianist to use octaves when accompanying the soloist. You can tap into that sound by incorporating octaves into your solo. To practice octaves effectively, keep the following in mind: 1) double stops are created by positioning the right elbow between the two strings, not by increasing bow pressure; 2) the thumb muscle actually inserts into the pinky muscle, anatomically speaking. Since octaves on the violin are mostly played by the first finger and the pinky, it's important to focus on relaxing your thumb muscle while practicing octaves so that the pinky muscle can be developed unhampered and independent from the thumb; 3) try to release finger pressure in between each octave so that the hand can shift smoothly up and down the neck of the violin:

Latin Scales

There aren't specifically "Latin" scales, per se, but it is possible to use the hybrid scale approach discussed earlier in the book, to avoid choppy key-to-key motion across the chord changes and streamline your improvisation by using a one or two-scale foundation. (See **Hybrid Scales**)

When I first started listening to Latin music back in the 70s, I was living in Guatemala. Learning how to dance well really got the rhythm into my body. Little did I know twenty years later that I would be the leader of an all-female Latin group, Pasion.

Latin music is a joyous experience because it is a blending of mind and body. Rhythm takes over and is absorbed. For this to happen, it is important to study, listen, and dance to the music. Syncopation is the key; the clave is that heartbeat and soul within all Latin music.

On the violin it is the bow that gives the swing and feel through phrasing and articulation. One must decide which notes to slur and where to use an up- or down-bow, which determines the accents. Because the violin is used both as a melodic and rhythmic instrument, it is important to have confidence in playing double-stops, and consequently, a familiarity with the chordal structure of the piece.

Playing Latin music has helped me understand and interpret all other styles of music. What's more, it has enriched my life through the tremendous enjoyment I get when the band is swinging, with both musicians and dancers having the time of our lives.

- Betsy Hill

SYNCOPATED NOTES SOUND OUT THE PARTS OF THE MEASURE THAT ARE NORMALLY UNACCENTED, AND ARE OFTEN HELD OVER INTO THE ACCENTED PARTS OF THE MEASURE.

Latin Rhythms

The use of syncopation and rests in Latin music help define its sound. Here's a montuno pattern (an open vamp section of a song) that uses octaves and syncopation:

To get into the habit of rhythmizing the bow while creating melodic phrases, you can improvise in the left hand while maintaining a rhythmic figure in the right hand. Warm up on an open string first to set up the motion of the bow, then apply the rhythmic figure to a scale. Then apply it to a pattern. For instance:

Here's a pattern that uses rests and syncopation. Try moving it through all twelve keys. Do this without reading the music, only using the notation below as a reference when or if you get confused.

Displaced Figures

You can create three- or four-note phrases and playfully altering their rhythmic emphasis and placement within the four-beat measure to create some very interesting figures:

Violinists are relative babies in the field of Latin music. It is an open playing field, an undiscovered country! There is so much potential here for amazing rhythmic phrases, interesting repetitive patterns across the strings, and double-stop work. This

It Just Is
by Michael Snow ©1995 Manic She-Owl Music

Rockin' and Rollin'

When the violin was first introduced into rock music by singer Buddy Holly back in the 50s, it was used as an acoustic classical instrument playing long tones with lots of vibrato. It wasn't given a solo voice in the idiom until later.

Rock actually developed out of blues and rhythm & blues. Both of those styles featured the violinist as a soloist. In addition to the players mentioned in the *Blues Fiddle* unit, violinists Sugarcane Harris and Papa John Creach figured prominently in R&B.

Today, rock and popular music use both the classical string section playing long tones or repetitious rhythmic figures, still seated behind music stands reading charts, as well as soloists using electric or amplified violins, such as Mark Wood, Karen Briggs, or Charlie Bisharat. The variety of amplified or electric solid-body instruments available, as well as the use of special effects like wah-wah, phase-shifters, and digital delay (echo), give today's player many choices in terms of their look as well as their sound. (Consult the chapter "Amplification" in my book *Improvising Violin* for detailed options.)

To play in a rock or pop band, you will need to follow a few simple guidelines, and have developed skills as a back-up artist as well as a soloist.

First, it's essential to create simple back-up lines that don't conflict with the lyrics when playing behind a vocalist. These lines can either consist of 1) a repetitive rhythmic phrase; 2) a harmony that's in sync with the melody of the song; or 3) a textural backdrop such as tremolo or trills.

Since there is no formal code of communication in this style (the way jazz musicians can depend upon charts with a notated melody and the chord changes, or classical players can count on completely notated scores), you will need to develop your reading skills to prepare for written charts, your ear training to prepare for artists who prefer to work by ear, and your knowledge of chords in order to work out background lines and solos that are key-specific. The good news here, is that rather than needing to know all twelve keys equally as you do for playing jazz, pop music tends to stay in E, A, D, G, C, and F. It also tends to prefer major, minor, and dominant seventh chords.

More often than not, a pentatonic scale is used (1 3 4 5 7) in these keys. For extensive pentatonic exercises, see my book *Improvising Violin*.

Since pop music is quite visual, make sure you look comfortable while playing, and try to avoid standing like a frozen statue. Aim to develop drama in your solos as well as in your stage performance.

We have already discussed the soloist's role playing backup for singers on 3-chord songs in the country unit (see page 62), and, like country music, many pop and rock tunes boil down to one or two scales the player can focus on for improvisation throughout the whole piece. You will need to work with the **Hybrid Scale**, the **Rhythmic Backup**, and the **Five Approaches to Improvisation** sections of this book to help prepare yourself.

It is also useful to be able to add or subtract vibrato at will, as well as slow it down and widen it, or make it hysterically fast, depending upon whether it is appropriate to create a lush environment, a cool saxophonesque quality, or an electric go-wild rock-it-out sound!

To gain control over vibrato, practice repetitively rolling each finger a quarter-tone under and up to pitch with the metronome at 60. Start with a quarter-note roll, then an eighth-note roll, triplet, and then sixteenths. Due to the limitations of notation, I have had to illustrate this as if it's a half-step roll, but the roll shouldn't be that wide, and the faster the tempo, the narrower the width should be:

Tremolo is created at the tip of the bow, using very small, fast bows that create a flutter. Classical players use a rhythmically measured motion, while blues players create more of a shimmer.

Mark Wood in performance with Celine Dion

The future of electric violins is happening now. Players have discovered limitless ways to indulge their own personal visions, ranging from their use of traditional acoustic 4-string violins to 7-string fretted self-supporting electronic violins.

- Mark Wood

Trills in this idiom aren't always the standard classical motion between two neighboring scale tones. Just as tremolo can be precise or like a textured shimmer, the trill can be created with a vibrato-like motion in the hand, making it tighter and faster.

A trill can also be applied between two pitches that are further apart, as in the example of a minor third. You can also add tremolo to the trill, and even move the trill up and down the string as you're sounding it out.

In *Sugarcane Rock*, you'll find a pentatonic run in the seventh bar, as well as a tricky figure in the eleventh bar. Take a moment and isolate both lines to learn the fingerings before you play the tune. Then solo using the chord changes.

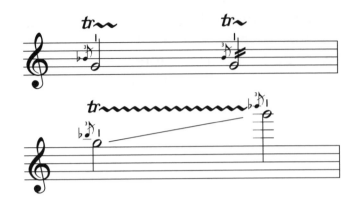

Sugarcane Rock
by Julie Lyonn Lieberman ©1999 Huiksi Music

Track Seventeen

Klezmanian Skies

The traditional music of the Eastern European Jews has been carried around the world, exchanging scales, embellishments, and rhythmic concepts with the Gypsies, the Greeks, and Middle Eastern musicians.

Most of the original musicians were wiped out during the Holocaust, but we know from early recordings that the expressive characteristics of the fiddle paralleled the sobbing quality of cantorial singing. Because the Jews and the Gypsies endured great persecution, they often performed together and had a rich exchange musically.

Celebratory even in its sadder moments, this music is hundreds of years old and has incorporated call and response; a tendency towards using an "oompah" bass line;

slides that swell into sobs; fast tight trills (using a half step from above); scales that use an interval of a minor third within

them; playing in high positions; changes in key or tonal center within the tune; and grace notes that lightly initiate the twists and turns of the phrases (called a *krechz* when played with the pinky).

Klezmer is highly emotional music, and klezmer fiddle playing, to my mind, is all about playing from deep inside. It can be modally and rhythmically interesting and sometimes even rather complex, but ultimately it's not intellectual music. Its essence is in how a tune wails even when its character is light and elegant or full of dance energy.

Klezmer ornaments, like the bend, trill, and krechz, are used to make something out of long notes that would otherwise lie flat, or to add emotion to certain notes -- much the same way classical violinists use vibrato. In fact, when I teach classical violinists to play klezmer, I ask them to eliminate their vibrato altogether, and whenever they feel an impulse to use it, to replace it with one of these klezmer ornaments instead.

Ideally, the melody should be played a little differently each time. This can be done, for example, by making a phrase a little busier the second time around (like turning a pair of eighth notes into a sixteenth- or thirty-second-note run); or by simplifying a phrase and turning it into one long, stretched out, bent note that adds some exciting tension. Taking basic, on-the-beat rhythms in the melody, and syncopating them to make them more energetic and interesting is also common.

- Alicia Svigals

Klezmer music is a musical, geographical, political map of the wanderings of the Jews over almost the last thousand years of European history.

Klezmer music developed in Eastern Europe as Jewish instrumental music used for entertainment and celebrations. It was a combination of the music of the Ashkenazic Jews who originated from the French-German lands (Alsace-Lorraine where the origins of the Yiddish language began), and the Jews who migrated from the Balkans (the Ottoman Empire) by the fifteenth century, who brought Greek, Turkish, and Arabic influences even before the violin existed. It was also influenced by the indigenous people of the Eastern countries.

Klezmer music is most influenced by the voice as it was used in the cantillations of our ancient texts, the most ancient being the Torah. So when we hear Yemenite Jews, Iraqui Jews, Jews from Central Asia (like Bukhara, Samarakhan, and Tashkent) who have been in the Diaspora (all the areas of the world inhabited by Jews who had been expelled from Israel and decided to never return), cut off from the influences of Ashkenazic and Sephardic culture, we're hearing what we suspect are these prayer tonalities that the ancient Hebrews, ancient Semites sang: melismatic (nonrhythmical) melodies. This is the base that forms Klezmer music.

- Yale Strom

The repertoire is filled with wedding songs, dance tunes, emotional prayers, and more. According to Alicia Svigals, "...some forms, like the *doina*, *zogekhz*, and the *kale bazetsn* are free-rhythm tunes which are completely improvised on the spot (drawing on some typical chord progressions and motifs) or are pre-composed but sound improvised."

The throbbing pulse of the music is often created by two fiddles playing rhythm (*fturkes*) with violin and clarinet carrying the lead. Bass drum, *tsimbl* (cymbalom),

horns, accordion, cello, bass, have all been used depending upon resources and location to support the music.

In Klezmer playing, the art of improvisation is often focussed more on embellishing and building lines around the melody than on creating completely new melodic lines.

To prepare for the tune "L'hu Neroneno," first practice the scale it is based upon:

This scale is an Eastern European mode called **Ahava Raba**. The seventh tone can be major or minor. Some sources refer to this mode as "altered Phrygian." The mode's Arabic name is **Hijaz**.

Now practice putting the notes into a pattern to help familiarize yourself with the scale, and to develop facility for improvisation. You can run this pattern across the four strings using the notes of the scale, and even practice bringing it up into position high on the E string.

Using the pattern above, apply a trill to the first note in each four-note pattern, and play the last two notes of each phrase slightly staccato (short). The trill is created by using a pitch that is a half step above the main note, and moving the hand as if to create a fast, tight vibrato. This is different from the classical trill, which is created by alternating fingers in a rhythmically measured fashion.

To help build strength in your pinky, try applying a **krechz** (a "pinkied" ornament) to each note of the scale:

This piece starts in a D tonal center, switches to G (first major and then G harmonic minor), and then moves to an A tonal center in the final section. With the exception of the two measures in G major (second section), all three tonal centers use the same scale tones!

According to Svigals, this tune is a **shabbos zmiro** (Sabbath hymn) that is at least a century old. Learn the melody first, and then try to add the ornaments. For improvisa- tion, use the scale(s) outlined on page 105.

K = Krechz; **B** = bend; **Tr** = trill using a half step

L'hu Neroneno
Traditional Klezmer Tune arranged by Alicia Svigals

Tango Caprice

A rage in the 1920s, the current repopularization of the tango by artists such as cellist Yo Yo Ma, The Kronos Quartet, and others, has helped re-establish this vibrant music as string-friendly. Even though when we think of tango music we think of the accordion's German cousin, the bandoneon, (brought from Italy by masses of immigrants in the second half of the 1800s), the violin was no stranger to the tango, as is evidenced by numerous recordings using strings, such as the 1926 group, Julio de Caro and his Sextet. Thought to be one of the finest tango band leaders of that period, Julio de Caro played a violin cornet (made by Victor Talking Machine Co.) and the band had a second violinist, Jose Niesco.

While the earliest recordings of the tango used brass bands, Vicente Greco's band, which recorded ten sides for Columbia in 1911, had two violinists; and Juan Maglio's quartet had one violin. Of particular note was the mulatto violinist, El Negro Casimiro, who was popular in this music before recording devices had been invented. Some other violinists of note from that era include Francisco Canaro, Ernesto Ponzio, and David "Tito" Roccatagliatta.

In the late 1800s, Buenos Aires, Argentina, had become a strong power in the world. The original Araucanian Indians and Gauchos (cowboys) had been driven off the land by the Spanish and the city had become a port. By the 1920s, half the population was from Italy and one-third from Spain, with French, Africans, and British, as well.

It was in the slums (*arrabales*) on the perimeter of affluent Buenos Aires (Argentina became one of the world's richest nations by the 1920s) that the dance style known as the Tango -- and its pulsating music -- was born. The Spanish-Cuban dance, the **habanera**; Argentina's version of the habanera, the **milonga** (incorporating improvisation with guitar accompaniment); and the African slave dance, the **candombe**, which incorporated wild rhythms, and energetic, freely improvised steps; all melded together into the semi-athletic style of dance we now know as the Tango. Of greatest interest to us, is the fact that the milonga was accompanied by guitar, paper-combs, flutes, harps, and **violins**!

Each style discussed in this book, except the blues, bluegrass, and bebop, is intricately intertwined with a dance style. As a dance, the Tango, tells us a great deal about how to capture the musical style: dramatic, punctuated phrases, interspersed with sharp pauses. Another important feature to the style is its incorporation of improvisation. It is thought originally that the unpredictability of the movements of the dancers sparked the same from the musicians. But as the Tango became the rage in France, smaller ensembles were replaced by small orchestras using a whole string section, and the parts became tightly scored rather than improvised. Originally, rhythm and melody were most important, and harmony was added in later in this style's evolution.

Alleviating improvisation and interaction between band and dancers led this vibrant form of music from wild abandonment to sensual but "controlled" complexity. For instance, the brilliant composer and bandoneonist Astor Piazzolla introduced chromatic harmony, a wider range of rhythm, and even dissonance to Tango. His compositions were controversial in the 40s, but by the 70s won international acclaim and set the standards for present-day qualities of this genre.

Tango music has a drama to it that is defined by athletic stops within the phrases with a rhythmic backdrop made up of emphasized downbeats:

It is common for a melodic phrase to dip back a note and move on up:

There is also a constant interplay between the instruments. The harmonic minor scale is often used, though many pieces move through several keys. I wouldn't call it a harmonic motion through chord changes, as the melody and improvisation may sit in one tonal center for quite some time; it's more like several actual key changes, and the new keys might use a major or minor scale, depending (see page 28).

Thick, constant vibrato as well as the use of a dramatic sweep (via a slide) up the string to a specific pitch destination can be heard in a number of tango compositions using violin.

You will also notice the use of a kind of chromatic circle dance around a primary tone:

Grace notes are common as well:

Here are a few popular patterns that might be used during improvisation that will give you a taste of this style:

As you prepare to play the tune, practice stopping your bow on each note of the G harmonic minor scale by relaxing your right forearm and pausing its motion. Try not to put a lot of pressure into the bow to create the stop, even though when you move the bow, you will want to really sweep it across the string to build dramatic flair!

Once you've played a chorus of the melody, then try improvising over the following chord sequence.

You can also use this G harmonic minor scale for improvisation:

Tangled in Tango

by Julie Lyonn Lieberman ©1999 Huiksi Music

Gypsy Lane

The Rom (Gypsies) share a common language called Romani. It is thought that the Rom are descendants of the Luri and Dom tribes of India. Many Rom were forced to leave India due either to persecution or war. As they traveled, they split into groups, and settled in diverse areas of the world, scattering again and again as discrimination forced them to move. During World War II, over 35,000 Rom were murdered by the Nazis and Romanian soldiers.

Music has always been a big part of the lives of the Rom, no matter where they've lived. Because both the Rom and the Jews were persecuted throughout the centuries, they developed a meaningful musical and personal relationship, often helping each other out, as well as performing together in Eastern Europe. The scales, harmonies, and stylization, as well as a preference for the use of the fiddle with either guitar, cymbalom, or accordion demonstrates crossover between the two groups.

The Rom brought singing styles from India (Rajistan) filled with melismatic melodies (many notes per syllable) not unlike East Indian Ragas. Both Jewish and Gypsy singing has a rhapsodic, expressive vocal quality that is echoed by the violinist.

Because the Gypsies have generally been a people without borders, some ethnic groups have accused them of stealing their music, and bear tremendous animosity towards them. I had a student in my World Music class at The New School who gave an oral presentation about her homeland, Hungary. She was vehement and her face literally contorted as she spoke of how the Gypsies had stolen the Hungarian scale and many of the tunes! Racially-oriented hate bias lives on in the next generation!

But all talented musicians drink in the music of their surroundings, and if they want to survive, they learn the local repertoire so that they can earn a living. Where can they find work? Weddings, social gatherings, cafes, funerals, town events. When it comes to repertoire, ethnic scales, and ornamentation, I like to think of the Gypsies in certain instance, as the archivists of the world.

There are many styles of Rom fiddling. The Hungarian style (Transylvania region) prefers syncopated rhythms, more composed lines, and playing in positions. It can also be very virtuosic, using fast arpeggios and runs. Southern Romanian fiddling (Banat region), which was influenced by Arabic music, tends to be slower, melismatic, and more improvisational.

Both styles tend to use minor keys, flatting or raising the sixth tone within the piece (particularly the Romanians) and switching from minor to major and back again section to section.

Klezmer and Gypsy violinists use the swells and sobs that come from Arabic influence as well as the repetitive phrases that build in intensity originating from prayer or expressions of ecstasy.

- Yale Strom

When a Gypsy tune winds its way into a frenzy, the tempo accelerates, and there are often repetitive passages that are played with lightning speed. Approach them slowly, with very short bows, and gradually notch up the speed little by little, staying as relaxed as possible. If any tension creeps in, bring your tempo down until you can sustain a feeling of release while playing fast. Try the following phrase in both octaves to practice this approach:

Gradual tempo changes within the piece, one scale ascending and a different one descending, deliciously luscious slides, all help create this incredibly expressive genre. There are more technical challenges involved in playing Gypsy repertoire than many of the other styles we've discussed. The music requires a knowledge of shifting and more complex uses of the bow, such as the bounced bow (including a series of bounced bows all on the upbow) left-hand pizzicato, and slides using a shaking or zig-zag-like motion as the finger moves up or down.

Let's isolate a shift to practice the difference between moving lightly and silently, versus putting a light slide into it. Sink your finger into the lower pitch, then release the string from the fingerboard before floating lightly up to the higher note. Now repeat this process, but this time drag the bottom finger lightly along the string. Release it from the string when you're about halfway up to the desired pitch:

While the majority of grace notes in Irish tunes come from a scale tone above moving down to the primary pitch, in this genre many come from the scale tone below the primary pitch, as well as from a chromatic step under, leading up, whether or not that chromatic tone is in the scale.

Trills are tight and fast, but the finger motion must be light. Think <u>up</u> to create this light touch, but don't increase the distance between your moving finger and the string:

The staccato bow is indicated by dots above the notes. Put a bit of separation between the notes.

Cadenzas are quite popular in this genre. They usually wind their way up to a high

pitch, using the chord tones of the key. Use light finger pressure, and practice your shifts slowly, imagining that a light breeze is blowing your forearm up the neck, bringing the hand and fingers along for the ride.

The Romany Trail moves through a number of tonal centers and types of scales. This is similar to a jazz tune, because, in a sense, you are playing over "chord changes," except that these scales do not correspond to our jazz chordal scales. In fact, only one corresponds to the seven modes we've discussed (A Phrygian: b2 b3 b6 b7) and one to harmonic minor (G harmonic minor: b3 b6). Some of the other scales come from Middle Eastern modes (*maqam*) such as the ***Shahnaz*** mode (b3 #4 b6), while others simply don't have names that I've been able to track down! You will need to familiarize yourself thoroughly with each scale in order to be able to create a fluid improvisation following the melody.

Gypsies (Rom, Romany) are a nomadic tribe who migrated from Northern India and spread throughout the Middle East, Europe, Eastern Europe, the British Isles and beyond. Gypsy musicians have historically made their living by assimilating the popular music of the surrounding culture and embellishing upon it, although authentic Gypsy music, which they play among and for themselves, is quite different and often more primitive. An exception to this is the flashy club repertoire of the Hungarian Gypsies, who composed and handed down through the generations a repertoire designed to display their mastery of the instrument.

The Gypsy violin music which has gained most acclaim, most notably Hungarian and Romanian, rivals and some say surpasses, classical in its exploitation of the instrument's capabilities. It employs the full range of bowings and left-hand techniques found in that genre and additionally such folk fiddle idioms as ghost notes, ornaments and slides. Players typically master expressive nuances, vibrato, and rubati, as well as harmony and ensemble playing, at a young age.

- **Mary Ann Harbar**

The Romany Trail
by Julie Lyonn Lieberman ©1999 Huiksi Music

Flaming Flamenco

While we can find a few examples of violinists involved in this incredibly expressive art form, there is no precedent for the violin in flamenco music. This presents an incredible opportunity at present for string players. And since violinists increasingly are drawn to this vibrant genre, it's time to incorporate it into the string world.

It's believed that Flamenco music was primarily developed by the Gitano (Gypsies) of Spain. The Gitanos arrived in Spain via North Africa in the 15th century, where they encountered Sephardic (Jewish) religious music, Spanish folk music, and Moorish (Arab) music.

Flamenco singing and dancing is intensely emotional and has been compared to the blues in expressiveness, even though the art form is quite different. The singer's voice is often quite low, hoarse, and nasal, using melisma (many notes per syllable); the guitarist creates highly rhythmic and melodic lines with intricate, fast runs. Both are accompanied by hand-clapping and foot-stomping. Guitar did not emerge as a solo instrument within this art form until the 20th century.

Playing Flamenco music gives us an opportunity to master odd meter and alternating meter. For instance, there are three meters that most of the pieces fall into: 12/8 (or 12/4), 4/4, and 3/4. The Soleares, which is made up of four 3/4 measures (or four 3/8 measures), forms a rhythmic unit of twelve beats, and has accents on the 3rd, 6th, 8th, 10th, and 12th beats:

```
      >        >    >    >      >
 1  2  3  4  5  6  7  8  9  10  11  12
```

We have already discussed the fact that the Rom (Gypsies) came from Northern India. In India, this rhythmic phrase would be thought of as:

$$3 \cdot 3 \cdot 2 \cdot 2 \cdot 2$$

Since the tempo of the Soleares tends to be quite fast, there wouldn't be enough time to count out the twelve beats, so the Indian approach to subdivision will provide you with an easier way of holding your own in this meter.

The melodies of many Flamenco pieces move within the Phrygian mode (b2, b6, b7) with a chord progression that resolves downward into the tonal center. For instance:

D7 / / / C / / / Bb / / / A7 / / /

Many of the violin techniques that we've covered earlier in the book, such as the blues slide, Latin paradiddles (string alternation), the full range of bow techniques and the chromatic circle around a chord tone in Tango music, can be applied to this style.

Harmonic Gypsy is not based on a traditional Flamenco form, but incorporates stylistic traits of the music. Improvising over it will require ease with the scale as well as the ability to play in 5/4 and over a structure that alternates meter between 5/4 and 4/4.

We will begin by simply marking out the 5/4 as 3•2 and the 4/4 as 2•2. Use the accompaniment, and start by playing on your open A string. Try changing pitch on each half or dotted half note maintaining this rhythmic pattern.

We will repeat this exercise using quarter notes on first the open A string, and then by changing pitch on each beat. Make sure you include the accents as they help define the subdivisions:

If you are on solid ground thus far, try applying this same exercise to eighth notes, and then melodic patterns:

We can then go back and repeat all of these same exercises re-subdividing as 3•2•3•1 to create another option for the basis of our improvisation.

As you edge out into improvisation on alternating meter, you can give yourself certain limits and certain freedoms at the same time by hitting, let's say, the open A string on the first beat of each measure and then allowing yourself to play whatever you want for the rest of each measure. This is to make sure that you don't lose your place within the five-beat phrase or four-beat phrase.

Once you can do this automatically, without having to count or think, you are ready to solo freely in this meter.

Use these examples to get started on each exercise. Then select your own pitches within the scale to apply to each exercise. You can use the exercises outlined above in any key and on any scale you want. These practice exercises are only suggestions. The point is to learn how to organize your practice time so that the rhythmic structure becomes a part of you. You'll know you've mastered it when you don't have to think consciously about it, but always know where you are.

I was raised in Florida and was in the school orchestra. I wasn't very good at sight reading and made my way to first chair by my junior year of high school just by ear. In 1970 or 1971 I improvised for the first time and never looked back. That's when I knew I wanted to play the violin. Up to that point I played well just because I could. When I improvised, I flew for the first time and never landed.

The blues, swing, Southern Rock, bluegrass, The Allman brothers, Jean-Luc Ponty, Stephane Grappelli, and Vassar Clements, were all a part of my early influences, but I still hadn't quite yet developed my own style. Whatever I could do to make a living on the violin, I did. First, I played folk-rock, country-rock, Texas swing, and bluegrass. Then I joined an eight-piece black band in Florida and that was another transition musically for me because I found out that this syncopated totally funky thing could happen on the violin. I could really groove on the violin. I was doing rhythm violin as well as playing with the horn section.

From there I realized that I could expand into anything I wanted. It was limitless. I got into salsa, I went to Europe and played with a Moroccan African-Latin group, and I began to travel around the world, absorbing different styles of music from the source. I lived in Rio de Janeiro, and recorded with Milton Nascimento and other Brazilian groups. I played five years with a Reggae band. After all that, there was a definite style developing. When I got with Lobo, he made me back him up since it was just guitar and violin. The real push was from the Flamenco style, from Lobo saying, "you have to do it." This was when I actually became a solo rhythm violinist backing up a solo flamenco guitarist. It became on-the-job training! I got paid to learn how to play in new ways. Playing live makes you much more of a musician because you really don't want to mess up in front of a bunch of people! I created a syncopated, rocking bow that has become the signature of the sound of Willie and Lobo. I became a rhythm violinist! To do rhythm, you can't hold the bow properly, you have to grasp it like you're going to "strum" with the bow because you can't hit all four strings at once; in order to play the chords to the fullest you have to be able to drop the bow on certain rhythms.

You need to have somebody play a chord progression with you so that you can just experiment all you want and throw everything from the past away. Listen to albums and play along with them — whatever turns you on; don't be afraid to sit in with groups; don't be afraid to do it even if you don't feel ready; don't be afraid to jump. Some men never stand because they're afraid to fall. Don't be afraid to try; once you do it, it's an instant transition. Once you learn to walk, you're a walker.

- Willie Royal

Harmonic Gypsy

by Julie Lyonn Lieberman ©1998 Huiksi Music

Segue into improv from this line or end tune by repeating first two measures as you fade out...

Playing Healthy

Playing Healthy

There is no one right way to play the violin. Each expert has evolved his or her particular left- and right-hand approach to playing and has naturally passed that on to their students. We are all, however, built differently. Muscle strength, arm and finger length, distribution of weight, and genetic tendencies are all factors contributing to body-type. In addition, there are differences between individuals when it comes to the number of hours spent playing, and varying mental skills that influence how much time or repetition it takes to master a piece of music. When you consider all of these factors, you can see that, technically speaking, what works well for one person might not work well for another, and may, in fact, create tension, discomfort, or injury.

Many players wait until they are in chronic pain, or can't function at all, before they seek professional help or make changes in their technique. According to the *New England Journal of Medicine*, almost half of all musicians experience playing-related medical problems. Awkward body positions in combination with long hours of repetitive movement account for most tension-related problems and injuries.

Musicians' incredibly high percentage of muscle-related problems reflect a flaw in our thinking and an imbalance in how we learned to play in the first place. Myths like "no pain, no gain," and teachers who force us to emulate their technique even if they have a totally different body type, or lifestyles that exacerbate repetitive overuse, with additional irritants like word-processing, are all contributing factors.

A balanced education, or reeducation, for those of us who already have trained for many years, must include techniques for healthy practice and performance. Whether practicing, rehearsing, playing at a lesson or a jam session, or performing, there are specific actions (mental and physical) we can take to maintain a relaxed, fluidly alive technique without damaging our bodies.

AURAL MEMORY: THE ABILITY TO HEAR AND REMEMBER MUSIC IN THE INNER EAR; BEETHOVEN RELIED ON HIS SPECTACULAR AURAL MEMORY IN ORDER TO COMPOSE AFTER HE WENT DEAF.

ANALYTIC MEMORY: THE UNDERSTANDING AND MEMORY OF THE OVERALL STRUCTURE OF THE MUSIC INCLUDING INTERVAL RELATIONSHIPS, KEY, AND CHORDAL MOTION.

MUSCLE MEMORY: A RECORD OF MOVEMENT PATTERNS RECORDED IN THE MOTOR CORTEX, CREATED THROUGH THE USE OF REPETITION.

IMAGISTIC MEMORY: THE ABILITY TO CREATE A MENTAL MAP OF THE SPATIAL RELATIONSHIPS, QUALITY OF MOTION, AND SEQUENCES OF MOTION NEEDED TO PLAY YOUR INSTRUMENT.

Muscle Overuse

One of the most prevalent causes of injury is overuse of the muscles through repetitive activity. Playing for many hours a day, even if you do it lightly, can eventually exceed the body's physiological limit. But, you could actually cut your physical practice time in half and learn faster because most physical practice can be accomplished mentally in far less time and with greater results through the use of imaging.

A lot of repetitive practice is often done while thinking about other things. This creates an environment that's conducive to injury, because the individual isn't paying attention to quality of motion. For instance, if you practice a passage while holding your breath, your muscles will remember to hold the breath each time you play that passage. And, while building muscle memory through repetition is important, it can easily be wiped out by nervousness or performance anxiety.

To develop a mental map of the music you are working on, you can use imaging. Imaging is a right-brain function. The right brain is in direct communication with the parasympathetic nervous system, which can connect you into fine motor skill coordination with heightened relaxation.

Sit comfortably, close your eyes, choose a piece of music, take a deep breath and relax. Imagine playing each note as if you were using your body the way you do when you play, except add in the quality of experience you wish to have and the form you wish to maintain in each hand. Don't actually move your body; do this all mentally. Stay relaxed, breathe deeply, and hear the music in your inner ears. This is the same mental process we use when we're daydreaming. We "act" out the activity mentally as if it were really occurring.

To image, you must draw upon your proprioceptive (spatial awareness), aural (the overall sound), and analytic (structural) memory of the music. This process immediately highlights which areas of the music you do and don't know. While imaging, you'll tend to hold your breath or tighten up on the same passages that are a struggle for you when you're actually playing, or you'll blank out on the spots that you always mess up. Imaging gives you an opportunity to train yourself to play those passages precisely with muscular fluidity and release, just the way you want them to sound and feel.

Each time you image the piece of music and then go back to play it, you will find that your mastery has increased, as well as your ability to include subtle details in the way you phrase and the way you use your body. The quality of experience you have while playing will also improve dramatically.

PROPRIOCEPTION: THE RECEPTION OR AWARENESS OF STIMULI PRODUCED WITHIN. FOR THE MUSICIAN, THIS EXTENDS TO CREATING AN AWARENESS OF MOVEMENT IN RELATIONSHIP TO TENSION AND RELEASE.

The Death Grip

If I tossed a ball in your direction and yelled "catch," your muscles and joints —without conscious mental direction—would know precisely how to "tune" themselves to the weight and speed of the approaching ball. If I yelled "catch this lead ball," a different setting automatically would be selected to accommodate the extra weight. Unfortunately, many musicians mistakenly inform their hands that they are playing with instruments made of lead; their tired, over-worked muscles never have a chance to breathe, and they fatigue quickly. Rather than experiencing a light, beautifully coordinated dance on the instrument, their playing bears more of a resemblance to a war of will.

To create a lighter touch, the best avenue for tricking the muscles out of their old "death grip" habits is, once again, through the use of images. For instance, you could pretend that your fingerboard is built out of soft, springy rubber. Or you could imagine that your fingers are long, light spider's legs and experiment to find out how far you can lighten your finger pressure yet continue to get an excellent sound. Sometimes it's useful to play extremely lightly for a few days, even if the tone is not acceptable, just to break old habits. Then you gently can add in just enough finger weight, (rather than muscular contraction,) to achieve the desired sound.

For the right hand, imagine that your thumb is a shelf (instead of a clamp). The bow just rests lightly on it, and the fingers drape over like the branches of a weeping willow tree.

Through repetition, the body learns patterns of movement in whole phrases. For instance, if every time you play a particular phrase, you hold your breath and stand on the sides of your feet, your nervous system will link those sounds and movements together into a "kinetic melody" and assume that configuration every time you play that phrase. Training yourself to use your body consciously as you play takes time and consistent conscious presence over time.

MUSICAL BIOTECHNICS: THE APPLICATION OF NATURAL FORMS TO THE PHYSICAL CHALLENGES INVOLVED IN CREATING MUSIC

The Stressed Wrist

Your finger muscles are in your forearm. These muscles control finger motion through the manipulation of the tendons, which run all of the way down the arm into each finger. When you flex your wrist in any of the four possible directions (up, down, right, or left), you are pulling the tendons tight. They will become stressed and unable to perform as well.

You don't have to take my word for it, though. Test this by keeping your wrists straight and wiggling your fingers, keeping them slightly curved as if you were playing the piano or typing; now flex your wrist in an upwards direction and wiggle your fingers; repeat this extended down, to the right, and then to the left. You will notice that it's much more difficult to move your fingers when the wrist is bent in any direction.

Now that you've performed this simple test, watch yourself play in a mirror and practice keeping both of your wrists straight. If you have a habit of breaking at the wrist while playing, it will take some conscious practice sessions to change this habit, but it's a change that will help you create greater fluidity in your technique, and protect you from injury in the future.

There are a number of common causes of tendinitis from playing the violin: 1) Repetitive playing at the tip of the bow (unless the individual has generously long arms) forces the wrist to flex for long periods of time; 2) pronating (leaning) the right hand in towards the stick, which locks the fingers into position, forcing the player to constantly bend at the wrist; 3) supporting the instrument by flexing the left hand to hold it up, rather than using a shoulder rest; and 4) excessive finger pressure on the fingerboard over long periods of time.

To protect yourself from developing tendinitis or carpal tunnel syndrome -- painful injuries of the wrist and forearm --use gravity as much as possible to do the work for you: release your arm weight into gravity during downward motion. Make sure you follow playing by stretching and strengthening the opposing muscle groups to balance the repetitive use of the hand and arm. For an in-depth discussion of these concepts, see my book *You Are Your Instrument*, or my video, *The Violin in Motion*.

TENDINITIS: INFLAMMATION OF THE LINING AROUND THE TENDON DUE TO OVERUSE, OR RESULTING FROM A TEAR IN THE TENDON ITSELF BETWEEN THE TENDON'S ATTACHMENT TO EITHER MUSCLE OR BONE. PROLONGED OR ABNORMAL USE OF THE TENDON WILL CAUSE THIS SYNDROME, RESULTING IN A TIGHT FIT WITHIN THE SHEATH AND CONSTANT PAIN.

CARPAL TUNNEL SYNDROME: TENDONS SWELLING IN THE WRIST PUTS PRESSURE ON THE MEDIAN NERVE LYING UNDERNEATH THE WRIST TENDONS, CAUSING PAIN, TINGLING, NUMBNESS, AND/OR WEAKNESS IN THE HAND OR WRIST. PERMANENT DAMAGE MAY OCCUR IF THE PRESSURE ON THE NERVE ISN'T RELEASED. SURGERY IS NECESSARY.

Muscle Balance

Muscle balance is an approach to movement that utilizes exercises which compensate for repetitive posturing. For instance, the constant forward motion of the arms and body to play on the violin can be counterbalanced by any kind of exercise that involves opening the chest or pressing the arms back in order to stretch the front of the body and strengthen or shorten the back muscles (which usually get lengthened over time from bad posture and repetitive forward motion.)

Any form of exercise is helpful as long as you don't strain, hold your breath, or do too much at once. Listen to your body and create or use simple movement exercises that tone your muscles and get your blood flowing. Remember to take deep breaths as you move to help mobilize your breathing and oxygenate your system.

In my book *You Are Your Instrument*, and on my video, *The Violin in Motion*, I have detailed muscle balance exercises specific to instrumentalists and, in the case of the video, string players.

Here are a few general guidelines to keep in mind:

1) Always warm up your muscles through walking, jogging, bicycling, or swinging your arms before you stretch. Picture your muscles like lumps of clay. If you try to mold clay when it's cold, it breaks apart. Warm up, and your muscles will stretch and change shape easily.

2) Avoid the use of heavy weights unless you aren't planning to practice that day. Weights break down muscle cells. It takes the muscles 48 hours to rebuild. We use our arms far too athletically to give them the chance to recover from a hard, weight-bearing workout. Use higher repetitions with smaller weights if you want to build arm strength. Always stretch and rest afterwards.

3) Try to avoid strength-training exercises that utilize your muscles in exactly the same manner as when you're playing your instrument. Seek the opposite.

CARDIOVASCULAR EXERCISE FLUSHES THE TOXINS OUT OF THE MUSCLES AND HEIGHTENS CIRCULATION TO CARRY FRESH OXYGEN AND NUTRIENTS INTO THEM.

STRENGTH-TRAINING EXERCISE, WHEN TARGETING THE OPPOSING MUSCLE GROUPS (OPPOSITE TO THE ONES WE USE DURING MUSIC-MAKING), WILL GIVE GREATER SUPPORT TO THE ENTIRE REGION.

STRETCHING ON A REGULAR BASIS REMINDS THE MUSCLES TO STAY LONG, AS THEY WILL TEND TO TIGHTEN AND SHORTEN FROM OVERUSE.

Rest and Healing

Rest is probably one of the best tools we have for healing. In addition to taking time away from playing to participate in a totally different activity and time to be completely still, you can structure rest into your practice time to serve a specific purpose. I call this "Constructive Rest."

Use constructive rest time to align your spine by lying on the floor and bending your knees. As you lie in this position, focus on relaxing and breathing deeply; meanwhile mentally play the music you were just practicing, adding in technical and musical aspects that were ignored during your "active" practice session. You can also come up with images for specific passages or patterns to try when you return to your instrument: turning your arm and hand into rubber on a particular string crossing,

becoming a 300-hundred-pound truck driver on another, and so on.

Another important aspect of the healing process is body-work, Alexander Technique, Feldenkrais method, massage, acupressure, and acupuncture, are only a few of the many resources available to you. You can find a full listing in my book *You Are Your Instrument*. We are fortunate to live in a time when these resources are available to us. Use them to increase circulation, enhance muscular relaxation, remove chronic muscular contraction, and nurture yourself. A body-work session teaches your muscles new "settings" which you can then bring back with you into your music-making.

THE KEY TO HEALING

WARM-UP AND WARM-DOWN

REST

TECHNICAL RE-EDUCATION

EXERCISE (OR PHYSICAL THERAPY IF NEEDED)

CONSCIOUS PRACTICE

Practice Time

Let's take a moment and review some helpful aids that are conducive to a successful practice session.

Is your practice space set up such that you can maintain good posture, have access to a mirror as well as audio equipment, and play freely without worrying about family members or neighbors? Is your instrument easily accessible to you and placed away from direct sunlight, radiators, or the inquisitive hands of a little one? If not, it is well worth the time to create a constructive environment for practice.

Now, think about where you place your focus when you practice. Are you listening? Are you feeling muscle motion and quality of use? Are you making music from mechanical technique, or from your heart? Are you using your eyes more than your ears? Or are you possibly thinking about something totally unrelated to music the majority of your practice time? If you are focused on listening and monitoring your muscles, then you are probably getting a great deal out of your practice sessions. Unfortunately, a lot of players aren't.

Think of your nervous system as the original prototype for a computer. It remembers everything you program into it, whether the programming was intentional or not. Neuromuscular patterns are formed so that you don't have to relearn every minute technical detail each time you pick up your instrument. These neuromuscular patterns also contain information like "alarm, alarm, here comes that hard passage…all muscle cells on alert…seize up, get ready!" or "this is the tune that he/she played a thousand times without ever listening to, or feeling the music, so let's just roll it out as if we were hammering a nail 50 times."

The best way to determine what you've programmed into your muscles is to tape yourself playing a tune, wait a few days, lie down and relax, and push the play button on the tape recorder. Pay close attention to what happens to your breath, your arm and shoulder muscles, and so on, as you listen. They will remember their "settings." Then you must go back to the tune and practice playing those tense spots slowly, with total relaxation, while breathing deeply, using a light touch, and making music..

CHECK LIST

MONITOR YOUR BODY AS YOU PLAY

REMEMBER TO BREATHE DEEPLY AND CONSISTENTLY

EXERCISE TO STRETCH, STRENGTHEN AND BALANCE MUSCLES

BE WILLING TO STOP AND MAKE THE CHANGES YOU NEED TO SET UP YOUR ENVIRONMENT TO SUPPORT YOUR HEALTH

Group Sessions

Playing with other musicians is inspiring, exciting, fun, and life affirming. It can also bring out the worst playing in everyone, and help build really bad playing habits. Group energy seems to take on a life of its own, often leading everyone to ignore quality pitch, tone, and ensemble interaction in favor of speed and volume. All musicians tend to bear down too hard in order to be heard or to hear themselves, and the subtler aspects of intonation and tone can easily be lost in the maelstrom.

If you play with a group of musicians who don't share your standards, or who aren't willing to make group agreements about pitch, speed, volume, and the like, you might consider finding a new group to play with. It isn't always worth it in the long run to go to a jam session and emerge playing worse than when you arrived, with tired arms and back muscles!

Sometimes simple agreements can vastly improve the group experience. For instance, you can use prearranged signals for changes in volume; you can layer the musicians in on a tune so that tempo and pitch are stabilized before each round of players join in; you can even prearrange the instrumentation so that layers of musicians drop in and out at designated points in the tune. Make sure you take frequent breaks during which you stretch and shake out, and try to come back into the session each time with fresh resolve to breathe, play lightly, and listen to your body's signals. These changes can enable everyone to focus on the quality of sound as well as the quality of experience.

WE ARE ALL UNIQUE AND MUST LEARN TO BE DETECTIVES IN SEARCH OF A TAILORED RECIPE FOR HEALTHY PLAYING

IT'S IMPORTANT TO STAY PHYSICALLY AWARE AS YOU PLAY

BREATHE: OXYGEN IS ESSENTIAL TO FUEL THE MUSCLES AND RESPONSIBLE FOR ALL HEALING

TECHNIQUE REHABILITATION: CHANGE YOUR TECHNIQUE IF YOU ARE IN PAIN BY BASING IT ON ANATOMICAL CONCERNS (ACCURATE USE OF THE JOINTS, TENDONS, AND MUSCLES) RATHER THAN BASING IT ON HOW SOMEONE ELSE PLAYS

EXERCISE: COMBINE STRETCHING AND LIGHT STRENGTH TRAINING WITH CARDIOVASCULAR ACTIVITIES

BODY WORK (MASSAGE, ACUPUNCTURE, TRAGER, PHYSICAL THERAPY, NON-FORCE CHIROPRACTIC CARE, ALEXANDER TECHNIQUE, FELDENKRAIS...): REPROGRAM YOUR MUSCLES THROUGH "HANDS ON" WORK

Resources

References

Companies

Chanterelle, P.O. Box 2235, Amherst, MA 01004

DunGreen Music, 65 Troy St., Mississauga, Ontario, Canada L5G 1S6

Faber Music, available through Music Dispatch (1-800-637-2852)

Greener Grass Productions, 6234 Rockcliff Drive, L.A., CA 90068

Kammen Music, 263 Veterans Blvd., Carlstadt, NJ 07072

Hal Leonard, (1-800-637-2852)

Homespun Tapes, Box 340, Woodstock NY 12498 (1-800-33-TAPES)

Huiksi Music, P.O. Box 495, New York, NY, 10024 (1-800-484-1333
    and key in access code 8400)

Jazz Aids, 1211 Aebersold Dr., New Albany, IN 47150 (1-800-456-1388)

Mel Bay Publications (1-800-8-MEL BAY)

Music Sales Corporation (1-800-431-7187)

PG Music (1-800-268-6272)

ProLicks, P.O. Box 31729, Seattle, WA 98103

Ridge Runner, 84 York Creek Dr, Driftwood, TX 78619 (1-800-FRET-PRO)

Sea-Cape Music, 1011 Hillside Mira, RR #2 Marion Bridge, Cape
    Breton Island, Nova Scotia, Canada (902-562-3433)

Sher Music, P.O. Box 445, Petaluma, CA 94953 (1-800-444-7437)

Books

Improvising Violin
by Julie Lyonn Lieberman

A companion to The Contemporary Violinist, Lieberman breaks down all of the components necessary to master improvisation, offering dozens of helpful tips on theory and technique along the way. (Huiksi Music. Distributed by Hal Leonard and IPG)

You Are Your Instrument
by Julie Lyonn Lieberman

A comprehensive, fully illustrated, 152-reference book designed to teach musicians how to develop a more effective as well as enjoyable experience during practice and performance, and how to heal existing injuries. (Huiksi Music. Distributed by Hal Leonard and IPG)

Blues Fiddle
by Julie Lyonn Lieberman

111-page instructional book detailing the art and history of playing blues on fiddle; chock full of tunes and exercises. (Music Sales Corp.)

Appalachian Fiddle
by Miles Krassen

Fifty-eight grand old fiddle tunes. (Music Sales Corp.)

Beginning Old-Time Fiddle
by Alan Kaufman

More than 40 tunes for the absolute beginner. (Music Sales Corp.)

Bluegrass Fiddle Classics
by Kenny Kosek.

Helps build your fiddle repertoire with eleven great tunes, breaking each down to detail the basic melody and several hot variations. (Homespun Tapes)

Bluegrass Fiddle Styles
by Stacy Phillips & Kenny Kosek

Careful transcriptions of over 60 of the most influential bluegrass solos...includes analysis and historical background...with accompanying cassette. (Music Sales Corp.)

Bob Wills Fiddle Book
by Gene Merritts (Creative Concepts)

Dance Folio(s)
A number of music books containing Klezmer tunes (Kammen Music Co.)

English, Welsh, Scottish & Irish Fiddle Tunes
by Robin Williamson

Over 100 tunes, this is an outstanding collection of the traditional music of Britain, graded from easy to advanced. (Music Sales Corp.)

Gypsy Jazz
by Polly Waterfield & Timothy Kraemer

From Russian and Greek dances to Bulgarian folk songs and Celtic lilts. With simple piano accompaniments. Delightful collection of fresh repertoire for the elementary violinist. (Faber Music)

Gypsy Violin
by Mary Ann Harbar (Mel Bay Publications)

Command your instrument's powers to move your audience to tears in the manner of the Gypsies. Includes practice tips, a helpful glossary, a short essay on the Gypsy touch and an assortment of approximately 50 annotated traditional tunes. (Mel Bay Publications)

Hot Licks For Bluegrass Fiddle
by Stacy Phillips
Over 450 bluegrass licks and how to apply them to your own solos...sections on double stops, upper positions, kickoffs, tags, fills, and a whole chapter on the ins and outs of "Orange Blossom Special"...includes insert record (Music Sales Corp.)

Jazz Violin
by Matt Glaser and Stephane Grappelli
Interview material and transcriptions of tunes. (Music Sales Corp.)

Latin Violin: How to Play Charanga, Salsa, and Latin Jazz Violin
by Sam Bardfeld
Transcriptions and analysis of solos in the Afro-cuban genre with examples of phrasing and examples of montunos. Available for purchase by winter, 2,000. (Published by Gerard and Sarzin, distributed by Music Sales Corp.)

Mark O'Connor: The Championship Years
by Stacy Phillips
Meticulous transcriptions of Mark's trend-setting performances at fiddle contests, written with Mark's help. Interviews and detailed analysis. (Mel Bay Publications)

Richard Greene's Transcriptions
Transcriptions of the tunes contained on The Grass is Greener CD. (Greener Grass Productions)

Roche Collection of Traditional Irish Music
Over 550 airs, dance tunes, and marches, with arrangements suitable for most instruments. (Music Sales Corp.)

O'Neill's Music of Ireland
A newly revised and corrected collection of the dance music of Ireland. Jigs, reels, hornpipes, long dances and marches, with an introduction on the history of Irish music and tips on playing with an authentic feeling. (Music Sales)

Ryan's Mammoth Collection of Fiddle Tunes
edited by Patrick Sky
This comprehensive book is a facsimile edition of the original collection published in 1883. It has survived over the years because it is one of the richest and most interesting of the 19th-century instrumental collections as well as a resource for students of American vernacular music. (Mel Bay Publications)

Salsa Guidebook for Piano and Ensemble
by Rebeca Mauleon
A sourcebook containing extensive information about the world of Afro-Cuban music. (Sher Music)

Scottish Fiddle Tunes
This collection of marches, reels, jigs, strathpeys, and other Scottish tunes has been compiled primarily for use by traditional musicians.

Selections from Moore's Irish Melodies
A selection of Thomas Moore's best known airs in easy arrangements. Eighteen favorites. (Music Sales Corp.)

Teach Yourself Bluegrass Fiddle
by Matt Glaser
This book is intended for the beginning bluegrass fiddle player and contains a guide to technique, solos, backup, achieving an authentic sound, as well as right- and left-handed playing. (Music Sales Corp.)

The Complete Country Fiddler
by Stacy Phillips
Authentic licks...300 solos ...interviews with top professional players...amplification of the fiddle...with accompanying cassette (Mel Bay Publications)

The Fiddle Book
by Marion Thede
Over 150 tunes, familiar and obscure, with lyrics. (Music Sales Corp.)

The Fiddler's Fakebook
by David Brody
Contains nearly 500 tunes from all the major fiddling traditions. (Music Sales Corp.)

The Fiddle Music of Prince Edward Island
by Ken Perlman
Celtic and Acadian Tune with historical information. Over 425 reels, jigs, set-tunes, waltzes, marches, strathspeys and airs, recorded "in the field." (Mel Bay Publications)

Trad. Celtic Violin Music of Cape Breton
by Kate Dunlay and David Greenberg
139 transcriptions complete with historical and musicological annotations and descriptions of the performance practice (DunGreen Music)

The Cape Breton Fiddler
by Allister MacGillivray.
A collection of photographs, biographies, and historical information with a few tunes woven in. (Sea-Cape Music)

The Grumbling Old Woman
edited by Donna Hébert
60+ fiddle tunes from New England, Canada and the British Islands, with bowings, chords and source notes. (Chanterelle)

The Klezmer Collection
by Stacy Phillips
140 pieces by the greatest practitioners of this East European-Jewish style that is enjoying a current world wide renaissance. . .transcriptions and detailed ornamentation (Mel Bay Publications)

The Compleat Klezmer
by Henry Sapoznik
Excellent historical information in addition to 33 tunes and a discography (Tara Publications distributed by Hal Leonard)

Western Swing Fiddle
by Stacy Phillips.
Over 100 transcriptions of classic swing fiddle solos from 1928 to the present. History and technique are explored. Contains a discography; a bibliography; and rare, historical photos. (Music Sales Corp.)

50 Fiddle Solos
by Aly Bain
Fifty minutes of recorded music by the world-renowned Shetland fiddler, complete with full accompaniments and a fabulous photo-filled book present the best of Scottish fiddle music. A must for the traditional musician. (Music Sales Corp.)

Audio/Video

The Violin in Motion
Take a 60-minute private lesson with Julie Lyonn Lieberman on video. Her unique approach challenges the age-old "do as I do," and offers violinists a physiological basis for building effortless, fluid technique based on individual body-type.
Sections include: holding the bow and violin based on ergonomics; bridging from a static relationship to one that constantly breathes; the motor cortex and music-making; body-type and technique; key technical tips; and an exercise program designed for violinists and violists! (Huiksi Music)

A Fiddle Lesson with Natalie MacMaster:
A 69-minute video. MacMaster focuses on five traditional tunes, demonstrating drones, double-stops, bowing, and embellishments of the Cape Breton style. (Homespun Tapes)

Bluegrass Fiddle with Richard Greene
Greene teaches a myriad of bluegrass bowing patterns, plus instruction in double and triple stops, the use of "bluesy" notes, funky rhythm effects, bluegrass slides, and tricks for playing fast. (Homespun Tapes)

Improvising Violin
Six hours of lessons with Julie Lyonn Lieberman covering improvisation on folk, blues, swing, jazz, and East meets West styles. (Homespun Tapes)

John Hartford's Old Time Fiddling
by John Hartford
A 114-minute video. Hartford discusses and demonstrates the bowing techniques of several of his fiddle heroes, and offers plenty of advice on dynamics, phrasing, articulation, improvisation and more. (Homespun Tapes)

Learning Bluegrass Fiddle
by Kenny Kosek
Two videos on bluegrass and old-time country fiddle will have you jamming with friends on your favorite tunes even if you've never played a lick before. His phrase-by phrase breakdowns make it easy to develop a strong repertoire of tunes. (Homespun Tapes)

Learn the Real Cajun Fiddle
A 90-minute video taught by Michael Doucet. Doucet breaks down the stylistic devices that give Cajun music its distinctive sound -- slurs, harmonies, ornaments, and more -- and teaches over a dozen waltzes, two-steps, blues and breakdowns. (Homespun Tapes)

Learn To Play Old-Time Fiddle
by Brad Leftwich
A 90-minute video. Learn to play fiddle in the real old-time style with this lesson in traditional fiddling. He teach tunings, drone strings and double stops, simple variations and several specific bow licks. (Homespun Tapes)

Learn the Real Cajun Fiddle
Six audio cassettes taught by Michael Doucet. Lessons chock-full of Cajun, Creole, Zydeco and old-time music of southwest Louisiana. (Homespun Tapes)

Learn to Play the Irish Fiddle
A 90-minute video taught by Kevin Burke. Kevin covers the basics of true Irish fiddle style, including rhythmic devices and variations such as grace notes, ornaments, rolls, double-stops. (Homespun Tapes)

Swing Fiddle
Learn improvising swing fiddle from Paul Anastasio. He shows you how to use forcing, chromatic movement, double neighboring tones, and syncopated patterns. (Ridge Runner)

Swingin' Jazz Violin
80-minute video taught by Matt Glaser. Glaser focuses on the playing styles of Claude "Fiddler" Williams and Stephane Grappelli, as well as technical tips, theory, and fascinating information on all aspects of swing/jazz music. (Homespun Tapes)

The Fiddle According to Vassar
A 90-minute video taught by Vassar Clements in which he shows you how to transform ordinary fiddle sounds into extraordinary one. You'll master more than a dozen of his trademark licks, plus slides, chromatics, double and triple stops, and more. (Homespun Tapes)

Texas and Swing Fiddle
Matt Glaser's six audio cassettes covering the styles of Benny Thomasson, Bob Wills, Vassar Clements, Mark O'Connor, and other great players. (Homespun Tapes)

Practice Tracks

Jamey Aebersold's Jazz Aids
Minor Blues in All Twelve Keys, Volume 57
Blues in All Twelve Keys, Volume 42
I Got Rhythm Changes, Volume 47
Swing, Swing Swing, Volume 39

Blues, and Texas Swing
(ProLicks)

Backup Trax: Swing and Jazz Volume I
(Mel Bay Publications)

Band in A Box
A software program that creates stylistic accompaniments in several blues styles, swing, jazz, and world music styles (PG Music)

Recordings

The Talking Violin
The only audio document of its kind in the world, this National Public Radio series converted to five hours on cassette covers the 20s through the 80s and is narrated by Billy Taylor. It contains over 50 improvising violinists.
1-800-484-1333 and key in access code 8400 in the U.S. or order via mail order: Huiksi Music, P.O. Box 495, NY, NY 10024 ($55 postpaid)

Blues

Randy Sabien
Fiddlehead Blues (N9323 Beaver Lake Rd., Hayward, WI 54843)

Howard Armstrong
Louie Bluie (Blue Suite BS-106D, P.O. Box 352707, Toledo, OH 46635)
Louie Bluie, Soundtrack featuring Armstrong (Arhoolie CD 470)

Blues Fiddlers
Blues Classics by The Jug, Jook and Washboard Bands (Arhoolie Records BC-2)
Stop and Listen: The Mississippi Sheiks (Mamlish Records S3804)
Mississippi and Beale Street Sheiks: Sitting on Top of the World (Biograph Records BLP01204)
Low Down Memphis Barrelhouse Blues (Mamlish Records S-3803)

Papa John Creach
Papa Blues (Bee Bump Records 310-426-0761)
The Best of Papa John Creach (Unidisc)

Bebop

Jean Luc Ponty
Sunday Walk (BASF)

Stuff Smith
Stuff Smith, Dizzy Gillespie, Oscar Peterson (Verve)

Joe Kennedy Jr.
Strings by Candlelight (CAP Records #924)
Accentuate the Positive (CAP Records #923)
Falling in Love with Love (Black and Blue Records 902.2)

Bluegrass

Richard Greene
The Grass is Greener
Wolves A'Howlin'
Sales Tax Toddle
(Greener Grass Productions)

Bill Monroe
Bill Monroe and the Bluegrass Boys (Smithsonian Folkways)
In the Pines (County Records/MCA)

Cape Breton

Natalie MacMaster
A Compilation
Fit As A Fiddle
No Boundaries
My Roots Are Showing
(Warner Music Canada, Rounder Records, and Greentrax Recordings)

Cajun

Michael Doucet
Mad Reel (Arhoolie)
Beau Solo (Arhoolie)
Cajunization with BeauSoleil (Rhino)
Cajun Music and Zydeco (Rounder)

Canray Fontenot
Hot Sauce (Arhoolie)

Dewey Balfa
Balfa Brothers Play Traditional Cajun Music (Swallow Records)

Dennis McGee
En Bas Du Chene Vert (Arhoolie)
Cajun Legend (Swallow)
Dennis McGee (Yazoo)
Dennis, Sady Courville & Ernst Fruge (Shanachie)

Wade Fruge
Wade Fruge (Arhoolie)

Country

Buddy Spicher
Cadillac Ray (with John Hartford)
Tennessee Jubilee (Rounder Records, compilation of fiddlers)
American Sampler (Flying Fish 021)

Flamenco

Willie and Lobo
Caliente (Mesa/Bluemoon Recordings)
Fandango Nights (Mesa/Bluemoon Recordings)
Wild Heart (Mesa/Atlantic)

French-Canadian/Franco-American

Donna Hébert
Rude Awakening (Flying Fish)
French in America (Chanterelle)
Soirée chez nous (Chanterelle)
Big Boned Beauty (RG2000)

Louis Beaudoin
Louis Beaudoin (Philo 2000 and 2022)

Gypsy

Taraf de Haïdouks
Taraf de Haïdouks (Nonesuch)

Virgil Muzur
Master of Romanian Fiddle (Auvidis)

Irish

James Kelly
The Ring Sessions (Rounder Records)
Traditional Music of Ireland (Shanachie)
Spring in the Air (Shanachie)

Martin Hayes
The Lonesome Touch (Green Linnet)
Martin Hayes (Green Linnet)
Under the Moon (Green Linnet)

Klezmer

Yale Strom
Hot Pstromi: With A Little Horseradish On the Side
Carpati: 50 Miles
Tales Our Fathers Sang: New Jewish Music with Tam.
(Global Village Music)

Alicia Svigals
Fidl (Traditional Crossroads)
Possessed (Xenophile)
Jews With Horns: The Klezmatics (Xenophile)
Rhythm and Jews: The Klezmatics (Xenophile)

Latin

Alfredo de la Fey
Tipica 73 en Cuba - Intercambio Cultural (Fania Records JM-00542)

Jose "Chombo" Silva
Sabroso: Mongo Santamaria Y Su Orquesta (Fantasy Records OJCCD-281-2)

Eddie Drennan
Lo Mejor de Tipica Novell (Fania Records PTH 55864)

El Nino Prodigio
Las Melodias de la Forties

Felix "Pupi" Legarreta
Descarga Cubana with Chihauhau Allstars (Palladium Records PCD-158)

Miscellaneous

Darol Anger
Heritage (Island Records)
Tideline (Windham Hill)
Fiddlistics (Kaleidoscope F-8)

Turtle Island String Quartet
TISQ: Retrospective (Windham Hill)
On the Town (Windham Hill)
Skylife (Windham Hill)
Metropolis (Windham Hill)

Eileen Eivers
Wild Blue

Old-Time

Bruce Molsky
Bruce Molsky and Big Hoedown (Rounder Records)
Lost Boy (Rounder Records)

Jay Ungar
The Lover's Waltz (Angel)
The Best of Fiddle Fever (Flying Fish)
Song of the Hills (Shanachie 6041)
The Catskill Collection (Fiddle and Dance Records)

Tommy Jarrel
Tommy and Fred (County Records 2702)

John Hartford
The Speed of the Bow (Rounder Records)
Aero-Plain (Rounder Records)
The Bullies Have All Gone To Rest (Whippoorwill Records)

Rock

Sugarcane Harris with John Mayall
USA Union, (Polydor 0704)

Mark Wood
Voodoo Violince (Guitar Recordings)
Wood Against the Grain (Guitar Recordings)
Guts, Grace and Glory (Guitar Recordings)

Scandinavian

Björn Ståbi
Orsalatar (GCD-35 Giga Folkmusik HB, Borsheden, S-780 40,
   Mockfjard, Sweden)

Miscellaneous Scandi
Musica Svecia: A sampler of Norwegian folk music including 25
   albums. You can e-mail them at <cda@cda.se>
Three Swedish Fiddlers: featuring Björn Stabi, Kalle Almlof, and Pers
   Hans (Shanachie)
Musica Sveciae Series. Nine of what will be a 25 volume series

covering all facets of Swedish folk music (Caprice)
Gubbskivan: The Old Mens Party. May be ordered from Foorlaget
   Allwin: per-ulf@algonet.sewww.algonet.se/jwinter/

Swing

Claude Williams
King of Kansas City (Progressive)
Live at J's (Arhoolie)
Swing Time in New York (Progressive)

Matt Glaser
Play Fiddle Play (Flying Fish)

Bob Wills
The Essential Bob Wills (Columbia Country Classics)

Tango

Astor Piazzolla
Tango: Zero Hour (Nonesuch 79469-2)
Kornos Quartet: Five Tango Sensations (Elektra Nonesuch)
Yo Yo Ma: Soul of the Tango (Sony Classical)

Julio de Caro
El Inolvidable (El Bandoneon EB CD6)

Stockholm Jazz Orchestra
Dreams (DMP)
Sound Bites (DMP)

Fiddle on the Web

Julie Lyonn Lieberman
http://members.aol.com/julielyonn
You can find links to all of these sites on my web site.

Turtle Island String Quartet
http://www.tisq.com/

Darol Anger's home page
http://home.earthlink.net/~derl/
This would be an interesting home page even if Darol Anger were not a fiddler.

Richard Greene
http://www.poky.srv.net/~martyw/greener.html

John Hartford's Web Page
http://www.techpublishing.com/hartford/
Access to links and old-time information.

Donna Hébert
http://www.dhebert.com/

Jay Ungar
http://www.jayandmolly.com/index.html
Info about performances, recordings, and fiddle camp at Ashokan

Mark Wood
http://www.markwoodmusic.com

Violink
http://www.violink.com/
Links to string related sites. Good starting point for any search.

Bowed Electricity
http://www.digitalrain.net/bowed/
The place to go if you are interested in electric fiddles and fiddlers who play them.

The ABC Home Page
http://www.gre.ac.uk/~c.walshaw/abc/
ABC is the notation of choice for fiddlers exchanging tunes on news-groups and lists. This site has freeware for Mac and PC as well as hundreds of tunes. Most of the software can play the tunes, generate MIDI files and print the score in standard notation.

Mark Chung's Jazz Strings Site
http://shoko.calarts.edu/~chung/jazzviolin.html
Lots of information on jazz fiddle, links and e-mail to performers, as well as string and jazz-related sites.

Canadian Fiddle Camps
http://www.bmurray.com/camps.html

Association of North country Fiddlers
http://www.fiddlers.org
Official website for old-time fiddle music

David T. Van Zant
http://www.seatac.net/dtvz/
Luthier. This site has lots of interesting links re: violin-making

Jewishmusic.com
For Klezmer books and recordings

Instruments for sale
http://www.NetInstruments.com/index.html#search
This is a listing service for people who want to buy or sell instruments. They list the instruments but are not the broker; the owner is the seller.

International Violin Company
http://www.internationalviolin.com/
Luthier. Supplies. Books.

Fiddlers on the web
http://www-openmap.bbn.com/users/gkeith/fiddles/Fiddlers.html
Stuff about a lot of great fiddlers, with some links which don't seem to be current or at least didn't work for me.

http://www.angelfire.com/ok/oibf/

1st Oklahoma International Bluegrass Festival

Fiddler Magazine
http://www.fiddle.com/
http://www.fiddle.com/links_camp.html
This is it!!! Great resource for info about fiddle camps. Be warned, some of these links are no longer active, but most are good. I spent a long time hunting for this sort of stuff and here it is all in one place.

Emma Lake Fiddle Camp
http://gpfn.sk.ca/culture/arts/fiddle/fidcamp.html
Fiddlers and events in Canada.

Listing of fiddle contests in the USA
http://www.fiddlecontest.com/contests.html

Elderly Instruments
http://www.elderly.com/
Used instruments, all sorts of music stuff, and CD's including some obscure stuff.

Celtic Connection Music Page
http://www.celtic-connection.com/music/index.html

Fiddle-Camp-by-the-Canal, Canada
http://cgmfiddle.cyberus.ca/fidlcamp.htm
Links to a number of fiddle sites.

Celtic music
http://www.ceolas.org/ceolas.html
Tunes, discographies, sound clips, artists, and more!

Cape Breton Music Scene
http://www.capebretonet.com/Music/
All you ever wanted to know on Cape Breton Music and links to more.

Shar Catalogue
http://sharmusic.com/
Supplies for string players.

Southwest strings
http://www.swstrings.com/
Supplies for string players.

Canadian Fiddle Camps
http://www.bumurray.com/camps.html

Association of North Country Fiddlers, Inc.
http://www.fiddlers.org
Official website for old time fiddle music.

SCAND@MATH. MSU.EDU
Scandinavian Music and Dance Newslist featuring discussions and news updates on activities in the US and Scandinavia

Newsgroup
rec.music.makers.bowed-strings
Depending upon your internet server, you should be able to negotiate to the server's list of newsgroups and type in this address. It will bring you to an interactive site where you can read and leave messages for fellow string players on any topics of interest to you.

Fiddle Camps

United States

Acoustic Swing Music Camp, South Plains College, Levelland, Texas, early August. Swing & western swing. Info: Joe Carr, Dept. of Creative Arts, South Plains College, (806) 894-9611, ext. 2272; carrmuse@aol.com.

Allegheny Echoes Workshop, Snowshoe Mountain Resort, Pocahontas County, WV, late June. Fiddle, banjo, vocals, guitar, dulcimer, bass, mandolin... Info: Snowshoe Workshops, RR2, Box 128M, Marlinton, WV 24954, (800) 336-7009; kirk_Judd@wvwise.org

Ashokan Fiddle & Dance, Catskill Mountains, New York. Three one-week camps in June, July, and August. Western & Swing Week, Northern Week, Southern Week. Info: (914) 338-2996/(800) 292-0905; ashokan@aol.com.

Augusta Heritage Center, Elkins, West Virginia. Five one-week sessions in July and August. Old-time, Irish, bluegrass, group playing... Info: Augusta Heritage Ctr., Davis & Elkins College, Elkins, WV 26241, (304) 637-1209; Augusta@augustaheritage.com

Blue Ridge Old-Time Music Week, Mars Hill, North Carolina, June. Fiddle, banjo, guitar, mandolin. Mars Hill College, Center for Continuing Education, Mars Hill College, Mars Hill, NC 28754, (800) 582-3047; cep@mhc.edu

Booher Family Fiddle Camp, Cottage Grove, Oregon. Five days of instruction, late June/early July, for fiddle, piano, guitar, and bass. Swing & old-time. P.O. Box 2234, Sisters, OR 97759, or call (541) 549-4305 (fax: (541) 549-8822).

Camp Bluegrass, South Plains College, Levelland, Texas, late July. Fiddle, mandolin, guitar, bass, vocal, Dobro; all levels. Joe Carr, Department of Creative Arts, South Plains College, (806) 894-9611, ext. 2272; carrmuse@aol.com.

Festival of American Fiddle Tunes, Port Townsend, Washington, late June/early July. Six days of workshops, jams, dances, and performances. Centrum, Box 1158, Port Townsend, WA 98368, (360) 385-3102.

Fiddlekids '99, El Cerrito, California, June 21-25. Day camp for kids ages 7-12. All levels. Bobbi Nikles, (510) 235-0370; bobbinik@aol.com

Gaelic Roots, Boston, Mass, June 20-26. Fiddle, banjo, mandolin, accordion, concertina, bodhrán, flute, tin whistle, guitar accomp., harp, uillean pipes, step dancing. Séamus Connolly, (617) 552-0490; email: connolsb@bc.edu

Jink & Diddle School of Scottish Fiddling, Valle Crucis, North Carolina, six days in early July. Info: 11302 Avocet Drive, Chesterfield, VA 23838-8945, (804) 778-7540; email: jinkdiddle@aol.com

Lark in the Morning Music Celebration. Mendocino, CA. Info: (707) 964-5569.

Mark O'Connor Fiddle Camp, Montgomery Bell State Park, Tennessee, June 20-26 and August 1-7. Several fiddle styles. P.O. Box 110573, Nashville, TN 37222, (615) 377-6064; email: fiddlecamp@pegasus-net.com

Michigan Fiddle Camp, near Flint, Michigan. Aug. 16-18, 1999. Aimed at ages 9-14. Some room for older campers and teacher training. Taught by Bob Phillips and Jed Fritzemeier. For information, contact Pam Phillips, Phillips Family Fiddle Camps, 734-429-0004 or wisenhymer@aol.com.

Milwaukee Irish Fest Summer School, Univ. of Wisconsin-Milwaukee. Third week in August. Fiddle, tin whistle, guitar, step dancing, harp, concertina, Gaelic... Workshops, sessions. John Gleeson, (414) 229-4923; Gleefam@aol.com.

Montana Fiddlers Association Fiddle Camp, Elliston, MT. June 6-11 and June 13-18. Fiddle, guitar and piano accompaniment. Info: Jeanne Buckley, (406) 323-1198; buckley@midrivers.com

Nashville Acoustic Music & Songwriting Camp (NashCamp), June 20-25. NashCamp@ aol.com, (888) 798-5012.

Ohio Scottish Arts School, Oberlin, Ohio. Late June 26-July 2. Fiddle, piping, harping, drumming, dancing. Info: Debbie Doty, (216) 777-8199.

Rocky Mountain Fiddle Camp, Aug. 15-22, 1999, in the Rocky Mountains just west of Denver, Colorado. Instructors include Liz Carroll, Jerry Holland, Paul Kotapish, and many more. Info: Mark Luther, (303) 369-1801; MFLuther@aol.com; www.RMFiddle.com

Scandia Camp, Mendocino, California. Mid-June. Swedish and Norwegian fiddling, hardingfele... Nancy Linscott, (415) 383-1014; email: 73111.2072@compuserve.com or Roo Lester: DancingRoo @aol.com

Scandinavian Week at Buffalo Gap, West Virginia. Late June/early July. Fiddle, hardingfele, nyckelharpa (313-327-3636) jbarlas@pilot.msu.edu

Stanford Jazz Workshop, Stanford, California. Early August. Jazz theory and technique with members of the Turtle Island String Quartet. Jim Nadel, Box 17291, Stanford, CA 94309, 650-327-0778; sjazzw@net-com.com

The Swannanoa Gathering, Asheville, North Carolina. Celtic Week, July 4-10; Old-Time Music & Dance Week, July 18-24. Info: P.O. Box 9000, Asheville, NC 28815-9000, (704) 298-3434; email: gathering@warren-wilson.edu

Valley of the Moon Scottish Fiddling School, Boulder Creek, California. Late August/early September. Alasdair Fraser & others. Terry Hallowes, P.O. Box 396, Cotati, CA 94931, (707) 823-3953; vom@monitor.net

Wisconsin Fiddle/Jazz Camp, Lake Geneva, Wisconsin. July. Aimed at ages 12-18 and adults. Teacher training. Taught by Bob Phillips and Randy Sabien. For information, contact Pam Phillips, Phillips Family Fiddle Camps, (734) 429-0004 or wisenhymer@aol.com.

Canada

By-The-Canal Fiddle Camp, Long Island Locks, Ontario (10 km south of Ottawa). August 22-26. Fiddle & piano accomp. Evening concerts and jams. Info: Loretta Fitzpatrick: (613) 231-2282 (work)/(613) 823-4565 (home) or Bruce Wilson: (613) 838-5687.

The Ceilidh Trail School of Celtic Music, Inverness, Cape Breton, N.S. Four week-long workshops in July. Cape Breton, Irish & Scottish fiddle. Also piano, guitar, and step/square dance. Before July 5: call/fax 781-544-3179. Web: http://www.ceilidhtrail.com

Emma Lake Fiddle Camp, Emma Lake, Saskatchewan. Five-day courses June 14-July 6. Old-time fiddle, guitar, piano. Info: Gordon Fisch, SCES, 2431 8th Ave., Regina, SK, Canada S4R 5J7, (306) 569-8980/Fax: (306) 757-4422; email: gfisch@gpfn.sk.ca

Fiddles of the World, Halifax, Nova Scotia, July 1999. Workshops/performances by fiddlers from around the globe. Info: Ivan Hicks, Phone/fax: (506) 386-2996; hicksi@nb.sympatico.ca

Gaelic College of Celtic Arts and Crafts, Cape Breton, Nova Scotia. One and two week sessions in July and August. Fiddle, bagpipes, dance, piano accompaniment... Info: (902) 295-3411.
Ivan Hicks Downeast Fiddle Camp, Riverview, New Brunswick, Canada. June 28-July 2. Fiddle and piano accompaniment. Info: Ivan Hicks,

(506) 386-2996; email: hicksi@nb.sympatico.ca

Meadowlawn Workshop, Bowen Island, B.C. Weekends in March and October. Lois Meyers-Carter, RR #1, K-13, Bowen Island, B.C., V0N 1G0, (604) 947-2440; cartmey@netcom.ca.

Orangeville Fiddle & Step Dance Camp, Ontario. Mid-July. Bill Elliott, 325 Broadway, Orangeville, ON, Canada L9W 1L4, (519) 941-5683; belliott@ headwaters.com; http://www.headwaters.com/elliott/

Wells Fiddle 'Treat, Quesnel, British Columbia. July. Fiddle, piano, guitar, bass. Box 4017, Quesnel, BC, Canada V2J 3J2, (250) 992-5776/5081.

Ireland

South Sligo Summer School, Tubbercurry, County Sligo, mid July. Fiddle, accordion, uillean pipes, harp, tin whistle, flute, banjo, bodhrán, guitar, singing, concertina. Phone: 353/71/85010 or 353/87-477817. South Sligo Summer School, Tubbercurry, County Sligo, Ireland.

Joe Mooney Summer School of Traditional Music, Drumshanbo, County Leitrim, late July. Fiddle, button accordion, banjo, concertina, harp, tin whistle, uillean pipes, flute, piano accordion, bodhrán, singing, set dancing. Info: Nancy Woods, 353/78/41213. Or write the Joe Mooney Summer School, Drumshanbo, County Leitrim, Ireland.

Willie Clancy Summer School (Scoil Samhraidh Willie Clancy), Miltown Malbay, County Clare. Early July. Info: Muiris Ó Rócháin, 353/65/84148 or 84281. Thirty graded fiddle classes.

Scotland

Alasdair Fraser Fiddle Course, Gaelic College, Isle of Skye. Early August. Info: Gavin Parsons, Phone: (0) 141 844373; Fax: (0) 1471 844383.

Glasgow Fiddle Workshop. Weekly evening classes. Info: Sara Melville, GFW, c/o Firknowe, 8 West Ave., Stepps, Glasgow G33 6ES, U.K.

Finland

Kaustinen Folk Music Festival. Performances and workshops. Phone: 358-68-8611-252; fax: 358-68-8611-977; folk.fest@kaustinen.inet.fi

Fiddle Horror Stories

Sometimes tragedies turn into gifts. That was my experience when, on a Sunday afternoon in 1997, my key broke off in the lock to my music studio and the doorknob was too hot to touch. A clanking, clunking and somewhat arhythmic radiator that always seemed to get louder while I was teaching had sounded its warning, but I hadn't heard its message.

Apparently the noise was a prelude to disaster. The steampipe to the radiator burst, filling the room with searing hot steam. The ceiling melted down, ruining my grand piano, computer and sound equipment, the floor buckled up, and when I gathered the courage to open my violin cases, having rescued them from the room first, the rosin was melted to the hair of my bows.

My violins were in the shop for several months. Seams reglued, new bridges and fingerboards, they came home sounding better than ever before. The manager took pity on me and gave me a new studio twice the size of the last one at a higher, but under-market rent. The hassle with the various insurance companies took eight months to resolve, but in the end everything turned out well. And, as a bonus, there are no clanking pipes in this studio.

- Julie Lyonn Lieberman

This happened several years ago at a bluegrass festival after drinking some kind of clear liquid from a mason jar. I was trying to demonstrate my version of Sally Johnson and stumbled into the fire we had going. After I put myself out, I didn't see my fiddle anywhere. Then I saw some weird blue-looking flames in the fire, so I got a piece of firewood and knocked the fiddle out of the fire. All of the finish was burned off of it, and the seams were coming apart. So I took it home and cleaned it up, took it all apart and got out the glue pot and heated up some hide glue and put it back together. I left the burnt look to it -- just put a real thin coat of spirit varnish back over it. It's ugly as hell but sounds better than ever.

- David Thompson

I practice with my computer and synth for accompaniment, so my practice space is in front of the computer with the synth on my left. There is a lightweight printer on a shelf alongside the computer. My violin books act like a bookend alongside the printer. Over time, music and music books accumulate on top of the printer. I am not a good housekeeper, and sometimes the pile gets quite large.

I was at my workbench working on a violin when I heard a noise behind me. As I looked up, the pile of books on the printer slid back behind the printer, pushing it forward. The printer fell onto the end of the synth which seesawed up on its stand. My violin and bow were on top of the synth and went flying. I didn't worry about the bow because it's carbon fiber, but the fiddle landed face-down. I picked it up and the only thing wrong was that a peg had slipped a bit.

My housekeeping in that area has improved significantly since that happened. The rest of the place remains a mess.

- Pete Schug

I was sitting harmlessly in my room, practicing Bach on my violin when the doorbell rang. Not thinking, I made my way to answer the door with violin in hand (luckily, I left the bow behind). Coming through the kitchen, I slipped on God-knows-what. My feet went out from under me and I fell backwards onto the tile floor. I was uninjured, seeing as the violin broke my fall.

There was a terrible twanging noise, and I have a horrible memory of the fiddle's body flying up and over my head, landing behind me. The neck broke off pretty cleanly and there was some cosmetic damage around the button. The bridge (I loved that bridge) lost the bass foot and the fine-tuner on the E-string left a 2" scratch on the belly as the tailpiece flew off sideways. The table separated from the ribs at the point of impact, there were some stress fractures, etc. On the whole, not a good day. Thankfully, the luthier was a friend. And, by the way, it was a salesman at the door.

- Scott Bailey

A metal-covered Bible fell off a shelf and zeroed in on the strings and unsupported end of the fingerboard. The Bible cracked the fingerboard, and ripped the neck clean away from the body -- all in slow motion. I'd only had the violin two weeks. After the first luthier, I wasn't happy with the sound (and he told me the fiddle wasn't worth the price of repair). The next luthier did a bang-up job, and the fiddle is almost as sweet as before. Lessons learned the hard way tend to stay with you!

- RLA Matheson

When I was in high school, my orchestra played at Biltmore Estate in North Carolina every Christmas. Near the main entrance, they have the Palm Court, which is a round area where they store plants in winter. It's got a marble floor, drafty, and it's a tight squeeze for a 50+

member orchestra, but so what. Free food and admission and a bus trip with your friends is good, right? I got a bit carried away during the Russian Sailor's Dance and overdid a down-bow, and when I tried to replace the bow on the string, I caught the fingerboard with the bow tip and flipped the whole business into the 2nd violin section, on the floor.

Surprisingly, the violin was fine. Stayed in tune, even.

- Danielle E. Martin

During a concert, a baroque string broke at the nut, snapped back, and smacked me in the face ... I was so startled I fell off my chair ...

I once saw a fourth-grade kid shoot a 1/2 size violin through a basketball hoop...swish!

- Eric Oehler

I took a round-the-world holiday and took my fiddle with me (not my best fiddle). Busking on Circular Quay in Sydney was cool to do. Airport lounges are the most appreciative audiences. They are soooo bored that anything is appreciated. All went well until the flight from Hawaii to San Francisco.

The fiddle was in the overhead locker, its box covered in fragile stickers. (I get a couple extra every flight and add them - eventually when the box wears out there will be this sort of paper maché shell left). They announced over the speakers as they do to open the bins carefully as things can shift. Immediately an idiot male in the seat in front of me decided to impress his female companion by opening the locker for her. He was underneath the locker, so he reached out over her head, around the underside of the locker and popped the catch. The locker door swung up away from him and my fiddle came crashing out, falling six feet into the aisle. It broke the bridge, sprung the top plate from the bottom most of the way round and caused a couple of small cracks in the top plate.

The idiot went pale and refused to give his name. Nice, honest people some of these Californians. Impresses the foreigners. He probably has nightmares that someone will sue him for damaging a Stradivarius, but like I said, it wasn't my best fiddle and it cost £38 to get it repaired. The airline was not very cooperative (mainly concerned with ensuring I couldn't sue them) but I did find a way to get his name. When I saw the repair bill I decided it wasn't worth chasing him.

- Laurie Griffiths

I bought my first fiddle at Sandy Bradley's instrument auction at Northwest Folklife in Seattle. It was an old German instrument of doubtful provenance, and had one thing going for it: it was as loud as a stuck pig. The tone was rather unrefined, and keeping it in tune was a struggle, but you could hear it on the next block.

I played this instrument with Seattle's Taproot Theatre in a production of "Cotton Patch Gospel," a bluegrass musical by Tom Key and Harry Chapin. It was a Saturday night, and we were smack in the middle of "Goin' to Atlanta," a barnburner (with a prominent fiddle part) that closes the first act -- the last song before intermission. Suddenly there was a loud snap -- my bridge fell over, and the strings came loose and went flying every which way.

One thing spared me from complete embarrassment: I'm also a viola player, and had been playing my viola in this show on a couple of numbers where I thought its tone was more appropriate than that of my fiddle. I sprang for the viola, and managed to switch just in time for my next solo.

An inspection during intermission revealed that the fiddle's tail gut had broken. This wasn't something I could fix by myself there at the theatre. Fortunately, most of the hot fiddle numbers in "Cotton Patch" occur in the first act, so I was able to get by on mandolin and viola in Act 2. Also, it was the last show of the weekend, and I had until the following Thursday to get the fiddle to a shop.

I bought a much better fiddle at the same auction the following year, and eventually got rid of the first one. But I guess the moral of the story is that it never hurts to have a couple of extra instruments sitting around.

You never know when your versatility will suddenly be called upon.

- Martin Stillion

A fiddler native to Tennessee lost his bow hand to a corn threshing machine (I think that's what you call it) about 15 years ago. He is very involved in the local music scene, so of course a way was found so he could still play. A prosthesis was fashioned so that the bow's frog could be clipped onto it. When he was performing a few years ago, the bow and attachment went flying into the crowd leaving a stub behind.

- Dean

I was getting ready to play for a square dance and found that my fiddle would not stay in tune. It was flat by a minor third or so when I took it out of the case (which is unusual for this instrument) and every time I got it up to pitch it would go flat, all four strings at once.

Ignoring that huge clue I focused my attention on the tuning pegs and made sure they were all holding well. They were, but the thing still would not stay in tune. About two minutes before the dance was supposed to start, the tailgut gave way. The little nut on the tailgut had been slipping (that was what caused the instrument to go flat), and it finally lost its grip altogether. The lucky thing was that the soundpost did not fall over. The bridge stayed in place because it's a Baggs System and the wire kept it from flying across the room.

So some volunteers who happened to have instruments with them played for the first 45 minutes of the dance while someone helped me jury-rig a tailgut. Later on I realized that I had installed that tailgut about ten years ago, and it wasn't new then! Now that I have a new one in place it's kind of a moot point but I always ask my repair guy to inspect it whenever I am having any kind of work done, and recommend that other people have theirs inspected too.

- Bo Bradham

I was a string teacher in Daytona Beach, FL for several years (oh...close to 100 years ago now). I had 36 violins, which I took to the 5th grade classrooms and taught the students for 45 minutes a day for two weeks. Then they could take after-school classes if they wanted. I had charge of 36 instruments. They were the super cheapo variety with equally cheapo cases. The cases got a LOT of wear so over the summer I decided to paint them. I tried to figure out an easy way to do it... and so... hung them in the trees outside my apartment. (Lordy! The craziness of youth!) Anyway, it worked. I spray-painted them, let them dry (trusting person that I was, no one stole any, thank goodness!) and put them back in the trunk of the car that the county provided for me. Except for....one fiddle which was kind of hidden up in the tree...oh my. Should I tell you that it rained that night? Should I admit that the violin was IN the case???!!!? Sad what happened to that poor, poor violin. I felt horror when I realized what had happened and saw the instrument sprung, separated, and totally ruined. It was long ago...and hopefully I'm wiser.

- Katie Bailey

One evening I was running late for a session and was ferrying items from the house. We had two cars parked side by side in the driveway. On my first trip I placed my black fiddle case on the asphalt driveway and returned to the house for another item. When I came out of the house I had to watch helplessly as my wife backed her car over my fiddle. She could not hear my panicky screams for her to stop and had not seen the case.

Luckily the case took the brunt of the punishment. After a new case, a new bow, and $300 of repairs (in 1985 dollars) the instrument was playable and continues to improve in tone.

Lesson learned: Apparently none. My wife drove over my fiddle, but that did not stop me from playing. If she wants me to quit, she is going to have to be more direct about it.

- John Beland

I have two stories:

1) Many years ago, I played fiddle for a square and contra dance held in a school gym. The band and caller set up our chairs and the PA at one end of the hall. It was CROWDED and the crowd was exuberant. One set near the band had a couple with the guy obviously showing off for his date. Every time the dance called for the couple to swing, he'd do so with great abandon and creativity. As they reached the top of the set, he grabbed his partner under the arms and swung her around, her feet off the floor and almost horizontal. He took out three mike stands. I grabbed for the one nearest me to keep the mike from smashing onto the floor. I missed and it went crashing into my fiddle, snapping the neck at the heel joint. I was furious. Tarzan was oblivious. Fortunately, I found a good luthier who was able to fix it like new.

2) Around 1973 I was playing with a touring band that did a mix of blues, rock'n'roll, bluegrass, and everything else. We played a show at a well-known university in St. Louis (which shall remain anonymous but whose initials are W.U.) with a bunch of bands who were quite popular at the time, so security was tight. You needed a special pass to get backstage and a second, different pass to get entry to the musicians' dressing rooms and instrument storage area on the second floor. Students manned the doors, checking passes.

We did our sets and went out to listen to a couple of the other bands. Late in the evening when we came back to the instrument area to pick up our axes and go to the hotel, we discovered that a few instruments were missing, including my fiddle. We searched the room and the entire floor -- nothing. We queried the student manning the door, who denied seeing or hearing anything. We reported it to the campus police, who really didn't seem all that interested.

At about 1:00 a.m., as we were about to head back to the hotel, I looked out the window into the parking lot and noticed a dumpster below the window and about 10 feet back from the building wall. It was a long shot, but we decided to check it out anyway. Sure enough, all the instruments were in the dumpster where the thief had pitched them from the second floor window.

There were a couple of saxes, including a soprano sax that had fallen out of its case as it hit, but they were miraculously unharmed. My fiddle was less fortunate, again separating at the neck block and getting a small crack in the top. I got it repaired and then spent several months trying to get the university to reimburse me since the damage occurred while the instruments were on their premises and under their control, but they were adamant in their refusal. I had to swallow the repair costs.

- Neil Rossi

Index

Resources for Musicians

— by Julie Lyonn Lieberman —

You Are Your Instrument: The Definitive Musician's Guide To Practice and Performance

Only a handful of musicians know how to create music in a fluid, pain-free manner. You Are Your Instrument is a comprehensive, fully illustrated, 152-page reference book designed to teach musicians how to develop a more effective as well as enjoyable experience during practice and performance, and how to heal existing injuries. Here's what over 35 reviewers have to say about this international best-seller: "…an exceptional title…well written…comprehensive…a must have…an invaluable vehicle for musicians who want to learn to use their bodies and minds more intelligently while practicing and performing…her six-level approach to memorization is worth the price of the book…it should be on the shelf of every musician who wants to play without pain."

Improvising Violin

Put Fire in Your bow! Written for the violinist who longs to leave the confines of the written page, Improvising Violin is a comprehensive guide to the art of violin improvisation in jazz, blues, swing, folk, rock, and New Age. this 132-page book offers dozens of exercises, riffs, stylistic techniques, patterns chord charts, tunes, photos, quotes and anecdotes, with a preface by Darol Anger.

Planet Musician

With·more than 150 world scales and modes, mental and technical exercises, and its fresh approach, this innovative publication offers exciting ways for players to enrich their own musical style by integrating ideas, techniques, and sounds from other musical traditions. Comes with a 74-minute practice CD.

The Instrumentalist's Guide to Fitness, Health, and Musicianship

With special guests Barry Mitterhoff (mandolin/guitar), John Blake, Jr. (violin), David Krakauer (clarinet), and Sumi Tonooka (piano), as well as physical fitness trainer Michael Schwartz, Julie Lyonn Lieberman helps you understand how your mind and body work together when you create music and what techniques you can use to boost that relationship in order to improve your playing. You'll learn exercises to relax and center you, breathing and stretching techniques, self-massage and warm-ups. You'll see and feel how tension negatively affects your playing and learn how to eliminate it. (90-minute video)

The Vocalist's Guide to Fitness, Health, and Musicianship

Julie Lyonn Lieberman and three highly respected experts – Maitland Peters, Katie Agresta, and Jeannie Deva – share valuable tips and hands-on tools to successfully counteract common problems faced by vocalists. In a simple, direct way, each offers advice and practice techniques addressing such important issues as breath support and control, vocal stamina, the causes of vocal dysfunction and injury, effective warm-ups and warm-downs, and the effect of diet and the environment on the body's ability to produce sound well. A lesson in vocal anatomy is included.(90-minute video)

The Violin in Motion: An Ergonomic Approach to Playing for all Levels and Styles

Take a 60-minute private lesson with Julie Lyonn Lieberman on video. Her unique approach challenges the age-old "do as I do," and offers violinists a physiological basis for building effortless, fluid technique based on individual body type.
Sections include: holding the bow and the violin based on ergonomics; bridging from a static relationship into one that constantly breathes; the motor cortex and its relationship to music-making; factoring in your body-type when building technique; dozens of key technical tips; and a ten-minute exercise program designed specifically for violinists and violists!

To Order:
Huiksi Music, P.O. Box 495, New York, NY 10024
1-800-484-1333 and key in access code 8400

— DISTRIBUTED BY HAL LEONARD and IPG —